Burnett

THE CONTRIBUTION OF RELIGION TO SOCIAL WORK

BY

REINHOLD NIEBUHR

———

THE FORBES LECTURES

OF

THE NEW YORK SCHOOL OF SOCIAL WORK

THE CONTRIBUTION OF RELIGION TO SOCIAL WORK

BY

REINHOLD NIEBUHR

PROFESSOR OF APPLIED CHRISTIANITY
UNION THEOLOGICAL SEMINARY

PUBLISHED FOR

THE NEW YORK SCHOOL OF SOCIAL WORK

BY

COLUMBIA UNIVERSITY PRESS

NEW YORK

1932

PRINTED IN THE UNITED STATES OF AMERICA

GEORGE GRADY PRESS   NEW YORK

PREFACE

These addresses on the contribution of religion to the field of social work were delivered at the New York School of Social Work as the Forbes Lectures for 1930. While their publication has been delayed for over a year because of my inability to prepare them for publication, they are being printed substantially as delivered. I owe a great debt of gratitude to the directors of the New York School of Social Work for many courtesies extended to me and for their forbearance in giving me so much time to complete my work.

The reader will note without any help from the author that the lectures represent the thoughts of one who is better versed in the field of religion and ethics than in that of technical social work, and the specialists in social work will therefore undoubtedly detect many omissions and discern misconceptions which a more intimate knowledge of the problems of social work would have supplied and corrected.

Reinhold Niebuhr

June, 1932

CONTENTS

INTRODUCTION

Objectives in life assume their greatest importance when the ways and means by which men live suddenly lose their efficiency. Ways and means have a day-by-day reality which sometimes leads us to confuse their smooth functioning with the end toward which they should be taking us. When they fail, after having served us well, we may realize that they do after all constitute only the machinery of existence. In creating and worshiping the machinery, have we lost sight of the objectives for which it was created? Do we ever formulate objectives with the concreteness which characterizes our development of the ways and means of progress?

Dr. Niebuhr's book appears at a time when the machinery of civilization is sadly out of order. In it, with his characteristic clarity and precision, he has analyzed the need of mankind for motivation and objectives which are beyond the creative power of human reason and technology. Readers will differ with his conception of religion and its part in human life; it will go too far for some; it will stop short for others.

But with his clear and forceful portrayal of the relationship between motives that lie outside the reach of reason and all sustained endeavor for the common good, there will be no disagreement. His discussion should widen the sweep of the social worker's horizon. Coming at a time when there is growing consciousness of a need to reëxamine the objectives and the spiritual resources of social work in a changing world, both its spirit and its substance should contribute to the confidence with which social workers take up this task.

This volume is the third to be published under the Forbes lectureship at the New York School of Social Work, although Dr. Niebuhr's lectures in 1930 were the second series to be given. The first series was on the Contribution of Economics to Social Work (1929) given by Dr. Amy Hewes of Mount Holyoke College, and the third was on the Contribution of Sociology to Social Work (1931) given by Dr. R. M. MacIver of Columbia University.

PORTER R. LEE

I

RELIGION IN THE HISTORY OF SOCIAL WORK

No society has ever been without some measure of charitable concern for its weaker members. In primitive society mutual aid may have been reserved for the members of the smallest kinship group and it may have been circumscribed by the strenuous struggle for survival which prompted the extinction of the aged, the weaklings among the young and all those whose lives could neither give nor promise aid to their group. But the natural roots of charity, the paternal and maternal impulse, sympathy for suffering, pity of the strong for the weak, were all present in the primitive community. The long history of man has but transmuted and magnified these original impulses. In the process of change and growth two forces have obviously contributed most to the refinement of the charitable impulse, growing intelligence and the progressive refinement of the religious spirit. It is not easy to determine the proportion of each contribution amidst the complexities of history: but it would be idle to deny the significance of either.

In the world of classical antiquity a growing intelligence was clearly the chief factor in refining social attitudes and perfecting mutual aid. Stoicism, which was a philosophy with a slight admixture of religion, was more potent than any of the religions of the Graeco-Roman world in mitigating the cruelties, enlarging the loyalties and extending the social responsibilities of that era.

In Hebraic antiquity a growing social conscience was clearly involved in the development of religion. The prophetic movement, beginning with the eighth-century prophets, made the needs of the poor the special concern of God and therefore a peculiar charge upon his children. They were to be allowed to glean after the reapers in the field.[1] The sabbatical year was enjoined as a kind of rudimentary bankruptcy proceeding which allowed the poor to be eased of their debts.[2] The weekly Sabbath, at first enjoined upon the basis of an ancient religious taboo, achieved humanitarian justification in the latter law.[3] Deuteronomy prescribed a second tithe for the poor after the first tithe for the temple had been taken.[4] It also prohibited the pledging of wearing apparel as collateral for loans;[5] and the prohibition of interest on loans was clearly meant as a protection to the poor.[6] The injunction that there should be one law for the citizen and for the stranger does not have the humanitarian significance sometimes ascribed to it, partly because the stranger did not actually achieve full rights with the Hebrew and partly because customs of hospitality in even the most primitive communities guaranteed certain limited rights to the stranger.[7] While some of the earliest laws in favor of the poor and the needy in the Hebrew Pentateuch

---

[1]Deut. 24:19.
[2]Exod. 23:11.
[3]Exod. 20:10-11 and 23:12; Deut. 5:13-15.
[4]Deut. 14:28-29 and 26:12-20.
[5]Deut. 24:10-13.
[6]Deut. 23:19-20.
[7]Numbers 9:14.

were clearly borrowed from the Code of Hammurabi, there is an undeniably growing emphasis upon the responsibilities of the community toward the poor and needy which emanates from the prophetic movement.

While Christian theologians and historians have always been tempted to heighten the contrast between the lovelessness of the world of antiquity and the love ethic of the early church, it is a fact that the religious spirit achieved a new triumph in creating tender social attitudes in the primitive church. Religious faith and imagination, coupled with the heedlessness which the hope of the imminent second coming of the Lord supplied, served to extend the social attitudes of the family to the larger religious community. The communistic experiment of the early church failed, it is true, but its brief life served to reveal to what heights of social responsibility men can rise when driven by religious passion. The fact that the love spirit of early Christianity, which began by wiping out the possessive impulse, soon degenerated into conventional charity reveals the weakness of a religiously motivated social impulse. About this we shall have more to say later. In spite of the early failure of the communistic experiment recorded in the book of Acts, Tertullian was still able to say at the end of the second century "We held all things in common except our wives,"[8] a remark which gives us a clue to the mind of the early church not only as to its virtues but its limitations. Origen quotes an apocryphal saying of an apostle, "Blessed is he who fasts to give to the poor."[9] The critical attitude

[8]Tertullian, apolog. Chap. 39.
[9]Origen, in Levit. X.

of the early church toward wealth partly inspired its emphasis upon philanthropy. Cyprian sold his considerable property before his baptism and gave it to the church and to the poor.[10] He also collected the equivalent of $4,000 in his congregation at Carthage for other congregations in need,[11] a rather remarkable bit of charity for that day, considering its economic resources. Clement warned against the perils of luxurious living, a warning which represented one of many compromises which the church made between its early rigorous attitude toward wealth and the possessive impulse so deeply rooted in society.[12] The widows of the early church were set aside for social and philanthropic work, and this practice gradually developed into the female diaconate, an institution still preserved in the Catholic Church and to a lesser degree in the Anglican and Lutheran communions, in the sister of charity. In the apostolic church the "agape," the love feast of the congregation, was used to provide for the poor. Each member of the congregation brought food to the common table according to his means and took from it according to his needs. It must be recorded that the leaders needed sometimes to admonish the congregation not to spoil the picture of perfect mutuality by eating all that they had themselves provided.[13]

Various religious motives helped to emphasize the love spirit in the early church—the inspiring example of Jesus, the sense of kinship under a common father, the

[10] Vita Cypriani, c.2.
[11] *Ibid.*
[12] Clement. Pædagogus ii I; iii 4. 7i.
[13] I Cor. II:20-34.

Christ-mysticism of Paul by which members of the church felt themselves united in "the body of Christ," and the sense of abandon which derived from the millenial hopes of the early Christian community. How much the sense of kinship with God heightened the respect for personality in the primitive Christian community may be gleaned from a word spoken to justify the practice of assuming responsibility for the burial of corpses washed up by the sea: "We will not tolerate that the likeness and the creation of God shall become the prey of wild beasts and birds."[14]

The philanthropic spirit of the early church was in part due to a natural sense of solidarity in a numerically weak community living in a hostile world. The emphasis upon hospitality, for instance, was no doubt due to the natural fellow feeling of members of a small sect living in a none too sympathetic world. Inevitably, therefore, the legitimization of the church with the conversion of Constantine ended some of the more charming aspects of the Christian spirit of philanthropy. But the social confusion of Constantine's period with its growing poverty was a challenge to the church which did not go unheeded. Naturally there was never a thought about the more basic causes of the poverty which incited the church to good deeds. The social situation was taken for granted. But within terms of it heroic efforts were made to relieve human suffering. Chrysostom answered a critic, who thought he spoke too much about charity, "Yes, every

[14]G. Uhlhorn, *Christian Charity in the Ancient Church.* Book II, Chap. V, p. 189.

sermon is about alms and I am not ashamed of it."[15]
Augustine, speaking of the futility of ritualism declared
"The true sacrifice of a Christian is alms for the poor."[16]
While there is some evidence that hospitals were first
organized under Julian the Apostate rather than under
Christian auspices, it remains a fact, nevertheless, that
the real development of the hospital occurred in the
sixth century and under Christian auspices, sometimes by
inspiration of the hierarchy and sometimes under the
influence of the monasteries.

The development of institutional charity proceeded
apace throughout the Middle Ages, even in periods when
the general condition of the church bordered on, or attained, complete corruption. In some of its aspects the
monastic movement was individualistic and indifferent
to all social problems. Yet it also represented a tremendous social and philanthropic activity. The poor were
fed, the peasant was instructed in agriculture, the arts
were kept alive and education was developed within
monastic walls. The monastic movement had its periods
of flower and decay which cannot be traced in this connection, but in its net results it bore a stronger testimony
to the social resources of the religious spirit than most
Protestant understanding of it has appreciated.

Not only the monk but the bishop was an agent of
charity. The social organization of the Middle Ages was
patriarchal. There was no thought of the reorganization
of society in the interest of a greater justice. Everyone,

---

[15]*Ibid.*, Book III, Chap. III, p. 275.
[16]*Ibid.*, Book III, Chap. III, p. 281.

accepting his station in life, was simply enjoined to be obedient to his superiors and charitable toward those who were less fortunate than he. The bishops had a particular responsibility for the care of the poor. While many bishops spent their substance in riotous living or wasted it in fruitless warfare, the history of the Middle Ages is nevertheless replete with authentic stories of good bishops who spent themselves in charitable enterprises. If the philanthropy of the Middle Ages, in its acceptance of the caste system of society, its glorification of the sentimental charities of the traditional "lady bountiful," and its general social conservatism, will seem to many a revelation of the weakness of religion rather than its strength in cultivating social imagination, it must be remembered that the medieval period had a static conception of society which made it quite impossible to think of social problems in terms of their progressive elimination. Yet it must be admitted, as we shall see later, that a religiously motivated social passion is always under the temptation of taking a social situation for granted and expressing tender social attitudes within terms set by a prevailing social system.

One powerful incentive for philanthropy in the Middle Ages will hardly appeal to the modern man. The profound otherworldliness of the medieval period and the preoccupation of the church with the fortune of the individual in the afterlife, united with a legalistic interpretation of the Scriptural observation that charity covers a multitude of sins, made alms to the poor a method of insurance against future punishment. So stereotyped became this form of almsgiving that it could be quite exactly computed how much charity would be needed to guarantee emancipation from purgatory. In a certain church council, it is recorded, a wealthy layman objected to the heavy exactions of the church in the interest of the poor with the observation that he had given enough alms to expiate three hundred years of sin. The Frankish queen, Fredegonde, who had hired murderers to eliminate a rival to the throne, promised high honors if they succeeded in their lethal enterprise and regular almsgiving on their death anniversaries if they failed, the latter promise being meant to insure their soul's salvation.[17] Naturally this legalization of almsgiving finally degenerated into pure commercialization in which rich sinners bought their way into heaven. In the more corrupt periods of the church, prelates abounded who wasted the perquisites of the episcopal office in riotous living, rich surplices and unnecessary church edifices, while the mass of the population suffered great want. Yet even in such periods there were usually some who remained true to the episcopal tradition which made the bishop the father and defender of the oppressed.

The vast institutional charities of the Catholic Church are a direct heritage of the spirit of the Middle Ages. The critical student of society will find much fault with this philanthropic spirit. It rested upon a static conception of society and it sometimes resulted in the romantic absurdity of regarding the poor as God-ordained instruments for the encouragement of philanthropy, thus placing the elimination of poverty quite outside the

[17]Cf. W. E. H. Lecky, *History of European Morals*, Vol. II, p. 237.

bounds of the Christian social spirit. Yet there was in the Middle Ages a religiously inspired sense of social solidarity and mutual responsibility, in comparison with which more than one modern era falls short. To this day the aristocratic sense of *noblesse oblige,* which still lives in some European countries and which is rooted in the spiritual idealism of the medieval period, has excellencies of social attitudes far superior to the ruthless indifference to human needs in the more commercial and industrial classes. The reverence for the value of human personality, the critical attitude toward wealth and luxury, the emphasis upon the love ideal in the Gospel, all these forces of Christianity had a real effect upon the social passion of this period which was so thoroughly dominated by the Christian church.

It was inevitable that the Protestant Reformation should destroy some of the finest fruits of the medieval social spirit. Protestantism protested against the externalities of sacramentalism in the name of a purer and a more personal mysticism, but it failed to recognize that sacramentalism breeds not only the vice of externalism but the virtue of appreciation for the problems of society. The sacramental church has a feeling for both the church and the state as a social organism which the more individual types of religious mysticism lack. Inevitably Protestantism bred an individualism which found it difficult, if not impossible, to preserve the best in the medieval social tradition. Moreover the emphasis of the Lutheran portion of the Reformation on "justification by faith" easily degenerated into a quietism and, at its worst, into a creedalism which depreciated every ethical and social enterprise as a revelation of the desire for the "filthy rags of righteousness." While Luther tried to substitute a new social activity, inspired by the Christian spirit of love without regard for the legalistic require- ments which the church had elaborated, it was inevitable that his reaction to the older forms of social and philan- thropic activity should destroy every vestige of the phil- anthropic spirit. Luther's ideal was that love should be spontaneous and should not be under either the guidance or the coercion of an institution. In trying to lift religious charity to this pure height he accentuated the weakness of the religiously inspired social spirit for it is always under the temptation of sacrificing effectiveness to spon- taneity and social usefulness to purity of motive. Luther himself admitted that his ideal did not produce results.

Before when men served the devil [he said] all pocketbooks were open; under the papacy everyone seemed generous and tender, men gave willingly with both hands and with grateful devotion in order that a false worship might be maintained. Now that it would be natural for men to be gener- ous and considerate in gratitude to God for the holy Gospel, many perish and die of starvation while everyone wants to preserve rather than share his possessions.[18]

Efforts were of course made to organize philanthropy in the various Protestant congregations for the sake of alleviating the misery of the poor. The general social confusion, resulting from the disintegration of feudal- ism, increased social misery to a marked degree in the sixteenth century and the plight of the dispossessed chal- lenged the social conscience of the church. In some indi- vidual localities rather admirable provisions were made

[18]Quoted by J. von Döllinger, *Die Reformation*, p. 323.

for alleviating the sufferings of the unfortunate, but no general system of philanthropy was established. The fact that Luther turned viciously upon the revolting peasants, who had erroneously assumed that the liberty which Luther proclaimed had some social significance and that the ferment of the Reformation might be utilized to emancipate them from intolerable social conditions, is an indication of his blindness to the social problem as such and of the social weakness of a quietistic religion. If Luther turned against the social solidarities of the feudal period it was with no thought of building a more just social order. He took the social order for granted even more than Thomas Aquinas and, toward the problems and iniquities of society, he reacted with alternating pessimism and optimism. At one moment he regarded "the world" as damned and in the next he gave himself to the naïve hope that if only everyone would follow the golden rule all things would be set right.

Incidentally it was in the very period of the Reformation that the Catholic Church developed its charities in forms which laid the foundations for its modern institutional enterprises. The highest development of its institutional program occurred in France where two great leaders, Francis of Sales and Vincent de Paul, particularly the latter, placed the hospitals under the administration of the sisters of charity; organized sons of charity; created institutions for foundlings, and, in general, exploited the social resource of religion for philanthropic ends. A man like Vincent is a good type of the combination of mystic and man of affairs which Catholic piety so frequently produces.

Not until the Pietistic movement overcame the barren-
ness of creedal orthodoxy in Protestantism did Protestant
philanthropy flourish again. It was under the influence of
men like Spener and Francke, particularly Francke,
that the Lutheran Church developed institutional charity in proportions comparable to that of Catholicism.
Francke's various institutions for the aged, the sick, the
orphaned, and for every other needy type of humanity,
are still functioning in Halle, Germany; and all over
Europe the marks of his influence may be recognized.
The Pietistic movement inspired Wichern to reclaim the
female diaconate for Protestantism and to place women
in the service of the church, both in the hospitals and in
the work among the needy of local parishes. The dea-
coness movement has since been an integral part of the
church in Lutheran countries and has developed institutional charities almost comparable to those of Catholicism. Still later Bodelschwingh organized Bethel bei
Bielefeld, a vast institution which began as a special ministry to the mentally diseased and then developed into an
institution for the care of every type of unfortunate.

Among the various Protestant sects, the Quakers have
always been known for the ethical quality of their piety.
For reasons which we can not analyse here, the Quaker
type of piety has probably produced more sensitive ethical and social attitudes than any other kind of Protestant
religion. Quakers were in the forefront in the struggle
for the abolition of slavery. It was a Quaker, Tuke by
name, who established the first hospital for the insane.
The labors of Elizabeth Fry in the interest of prison
reform are matters of general history. Incidentally a

Booth, with his combination of evangelistic zeal and social service in the Salvation Army; and more recently Canon Barnett who pioneered in social settlements at Toynbee Hall. In practically every case it is philanthropy rather than social change which these religious idealists envisaged, two of them, Shaftesbury and Wilberforce, being particularly marked in their social conservatism outside of their special field of interest.

The secularization of social work, which achieved a higher degree of consistency in England than on the Continent, reached its culmination in America, except of course in Catholic America, in which the old traditions have been preserved unimpaired. How powerful these traditions are may best be gauged in France where the Revolution destroyed the power of the church without impairing the relationship between church and charity, the institutions of charity being still prevailingly under church auspices. The fact that secularization was most consistently developed in America gives us a very ready clue to its causes. America is prevailingly Protestant, and Puritan sects of Protestantism are dominant in its life. In contrast to both Catholicism and the semi-Catholicism of Anglicanism and Lutheranism, these sects had less regard for the total social problem of society because they regarded themselves as voluntary associations rather than as the religious organization of the total community. In America this was accentuated by the fact that the ideal of the voluntary religious organization, "the free church in the free state," was written into the very Constitution. Furthermore the absence of any one prevailing church tradition and the multifarious character of our immigration developed on American soil the denominationalism of Protestantism in its richest variety. The disunity of the church made secularization of social work imperative. There are enough limitations in a religiously inspired institutional charity to justify the conclusion that secularization is a desirable end. Our interest for the moment is not to weigh that judgment, but merely to record the fact that the church is the mother of organized charity, though a mother who has lost the loyalty of this as of many of her other children. The anarchic disunity of Protestantism makes the secularization of social work inevitable, even if it were not desirable. It is quite impossible, in grappling with the increasingly complex problems of an urban civilization, to use an instrument as divided as the Protestant Church. Nevertheless there are creditable institutions of charity, particularly hospitals, under Protestant auspices. Churches in America which have a continental origin still indulge in more ambitious institutional ventures than the "sects" of Nonconformist English tradition.

Whatever the weaknesses of institutional charity from the perspective of the total ethical and social problems of a society, it is difficult to escape the conclusion that the superiority of Catholicism over Protestantism in this field of religious activity represents a real virtue of Catholicism—its sense of responsibility for the social realities and the high type of ethical insight developed by the monastic movement. Lutheran Protestantism tends to be Quietistic rather than socially active and the superior social activity of the churches of Calvinism stops short of deep concern for the most needy. Calvinism has never been able to overcome the temptation to regard poverty as a consequence of laziness and vice, and therefore to leave the poor and the needy to the punishment which a righteous God has inflicted upon them.

The increasing tendency toward secularization in social work has yet another cause which, if fully understood, does not discredit religion as an inspirer of social activity. Frequently the secular state assumes responsibility for social services once rendered by the church, simply because the church anticipated the conscience of the state in regard to these services and the state only gradually came to recognize its responsibilities. The care of the sick was first undertaken by the church, but the state recognized this care as a responsibility of the total community. In the same manner the church pioneered in institutions for the mentally defective until society, as such, assumed the burden of this class of unfortunates. Orphans were first provided for in church institutions. Mothers' pensions and child-placing agencies, either semiofficial or under state auspices, now care for the orphaned child more adequately than any institution could. Institutions for the aged are still necessary because the modern state, at least our own American state, has not yet recognized the social necessity of old-age pensions.

The general tendency of society to take over social services which were once the province of the church, or of some other voluntary agency, is so logical that it might be developed into a principle. The principle is that it is the business of the church and other idealistic institutions to pioneer in the field of social work and to discover obligations which society, as such, has not yet recognized, but to yield these to society as soon as there is a general recognition of society's responsibility therefor. In every morally vital society there is a possibility of experimentation in new types of social work and of discovery of new and wider social responsibilities. This is the proper province of institutions based on an ideal and of voluntary social agencies. At the present moment, birth-control clinics and clinics for psychiatric treatment might properly come within the province of voluntary charities, since they represent types of social services the legitimacy of which society as such has not yet generally recognized. Naturally there are some forms of social service which ought to be abolished entirely and which exist only because society creates, by limitations and injustices in its economic structure, the needy to whom they minister. About this we will have more to say later.

Our review of the relation of religion to social work seems to offer indubitable proof that religion does create a conscience which is quick to understand social need and ready to move toward its alleviation, if not ready to work for its elimination. In a society in which a great deal of social need is eliminated by the economic reorganization of society itself, and in which the care of the subnormal and the defective is also under the control of the state, the age-old impulses of religion must express themselves less officially. This offers a problem to which we will address ourselves in a later lecture.

II

THE LIMITATIONS OF A RELIGIOUSLY
INSPIRED PHILANTHROPY

Religion, we have seen, is fruitful of social attitudes, and creates a moral sensitivity, resulting naturally in deeds of kindness and helpfulness to those who are in need. It has not always produced these fruits, of course. In Buddhism, for instance, a religion which rivals Christianity in the purity of its spirituality, the strong emphasis upon love is negated by the profound pessimism which regards all desire as evil and which results therefore in sympathy for, but not in helpfulness toward, the needs of the unfortunate. In Christianity itself there are forces of creedalism and of Quietism, which, if they become dominant, destroy or strongly qualify the ethical and social passions created by it. Nevertheless the record clearly proves that religion—certainly the Christian religion in all of its varied forms—encourages sensitivity to the needs of others and usually organizes the tender impulses engendered by it into institutional forms of helpfulness.

There was a suggestion in our first lecture that religious philanthropy reveals some weaknesses which seem to spring from the limitations of religion itself. These we must study and consider further. The most obvious weakness of religion in social action is that it seems always to create a spirit of generosity within terms of a social system, without developing an idealism vigorous or astute enough to condemn the social system in the name of a higher justice. Religion, in other words, is more fruitful of philanthropy than of social justice. It might be claimed that this tendency reveals not so much a weakness of religion, as a natural limitation of the human imagination. The average man does not have an intelligence keen enough to question the social structure in which he stands. Since it is older than he, he easily lends himself to the illusion that it is eternal and immutable. He has not seen the historical processes which gave it birth, and he has little confidence therefore in the possibility of its transmutation. Since religion, however, always carries with it a sense of the absolute which prompts it to condemn present realities from the perspective of perfection and to dream of a day when perfect love and justice will be attained, there must be some special reason for its frequent easy and uncritical acceptance of the social situation in which it exists.

Frequently it is religion's sense of the absolute that betrays it into social conservatism at the very moment in which it regards the contemporary social structure critically. The absolute perfection, the holiness of God, the ideal of the Kingdom of God, which are religion's standard of comparison with present realities, betray it into a complete pessimism as to the possibility of saving the world. The world of injustice is taken for granted. It was destined to be evil by the fall of man and it will not be saved except as it is saved by divine intervention. The best a Christian can do is to live in terms of love within the system. Practically, this meant very frequently that the religious ideal of love was realized only in religious terms and within the religious community and no effort was made to apply it to the secular social situation. The attitude of the early church toward slavery is a case in point.

Slavery was taken for granted, though frequently Christian slaves were manumitted by Christian masters. The conflict between the ethical radicalism and the religious conservatism of early Christianity is clearly seen in Paul's letter to Philemon, in which he counsels the master not only to take back the runaway slave Onesimus, but to receive him as a brother in Christ and as his (Paul's) son, since he had begotten him in Christ, *i.e.*, converted him to Christianity. In the same spirit, slaves could be members and officeholders in the early Christian churches, a right which was not abrogated until the time of Gregory. Though some masters freed their slaves, and though the church gave them rights greater than those enjoyed in the state, the attitude of some Christian masters toward their slaves could not have been very considerate, or we would not find the church in the time of Polycarp ordaining that a master who whips his slave so severely as to cause his death shall be excommunicated for seven years.[1]

Polycarp incidentally reveals another root of the social conservatism of Christianity when he admonishes slaves not to seek their freedom lest they betray thereby their slavery to the lusts of the flesh. A strong emphasis upon

[1] Cf. also Lecky, *History of European Morals*, Vol. II, pp. 66 f.

the doctrine of self-sacrifice has again and again tempted the church into a critical attitude toward the assertion of rights on the part of the dispossessed, on the ground that this represented an expression of selfishness. The inclination to interpret the nonresistance of Christ as an example for all those who suffer from social injustice appears again and again in Christian history, and betrays the church into an acceptance of social injustice because injustice can not be resisted without the assertion of self-interest and the return of evil for evil. The logic of this position is perfectly stated in I Peter 2:18-19, 21:

> Servant, be subject to your masters with all fear; not only to the good and gentle, but also to the froward.
>
> For this is thankworthy, if a man for conscience toward God endure grief, suffering wrongfully. . . .
>
> For even hereunto were ye called: because Christ also suffered for us, leaving us an example, that ye should follow his steps.

Luther avails himself of the same argument in dealing with the revolt of the peasants after the Reformation. It reveals one of the dangerous and difficult characteristics of religion, *i.e.* the absolute character of its idealism, legitimate as a guide to personal conduct, but of doubtful value as a basis for social and political strategy. Clergymen who today oppose strike activities on the part of organized labor, because they regard such strategy as a violation of the law of love, are in the same moral confusion. It is a rather tragic paradox that the Christian conscience should so frequently suffer injustice to continue, because it knows of no way to resist it without violating its perfectionist ideal of love.

Another root of the social conservatism of religion, which tempts it to practice charity within the limitations of a social system without raising ultimate questions about the justice of the system itself, is the natural determinism of religion. To the religious imagination, God is at one moment the ideal toward which all things must strive and by comparison with which all contemporary social standards are convicted of inadequacy; and in the next moment he is the omnipotent creator of all things, whose power and wisdom guarantees the goodness of existing social organizations. Paul put the logic of this determinism clearly in Romans 13:1-2:

> Let every soul be subject unto the higher powers. For there is no power but of God; the powers that be are ordained of God. Whosoever therefore resisteth the power, resisteth the ordinance of God.

The doctrine of this word of Paul was potent in justifying the accommodation of the early church to the state, once the millennial hopes had faded and it became necessary to come to terms with the Roman Empire. It is probably safe to say that no single word of Scripture has had a more conservative influence than this fateful word of Paul's. In the Middle Ages it buttressed and justified the feudal order. The social conservatism of medieval society did not derive purely from this religious conservatism, for it inhered in the static conception of society which prevailed at that time; but it provided the church with a logic by which it could hallow the rule of force which the state maintained even while it claimed to be itself based upon a higher law, the law of love. In the period of the Reformation, it provided Luther a nice sanctification of his subservience to the German princes. No one knows how frequently this Pauline doctrine was invoked during the late World War.

It must not be assumed, however, that the tendencies toward determinism in the history of Christianity rest upon a single scriptural phrase. The idea that social and political arrangements must be virtuous because they exist under an omnipotent God who could change them if he would, grows out of a natural inclination in the very heart of religion, the inclination to aggrandize the object of worship, God, until it becomes coextensive with the whole of reality. A variant of this doctrine was to assume that the present status of society was ordained of God after the fall, to deal with man's sinful condition. Thus the post-apostolic church borrowed the idea of natural law from Stoicism, and found both imperialism and slavery sanctioned by this natural law which God had ordained for men in their state of sin. The idea of a natural law, lower and yet no less God-ordained than the law of the Gospel, persisted throughout the Middle Ages and provided the church with a basis for that curious dualism by which it sanctified, and yet claimed superiority over, the state.

Religious determinism has again and again betrayed the institutions of religion into an attitude of indifference toward the miseries of the poor, the argument being that God has ordained poverty, as well as the fate of the particular individuals who suffer from its deprivations. In Nelson's "Address to Persons of Quality," written during the reign of Queen Anne, we read: "Is it not indeed the infinite God who has made some persons rich and great and appointed the poor and needy to work day and night for their service?"[2] The author raises the question, why God should have ordained this inequality; but being unable to answer it, comes to the conclusion that it belongs to the inscrutable mysteries of God which he cannot penetrate further than to realize that it is good for the rich to be rich and for the poor to be poor, but that it is not good for the poor to become rich. The literature of our own Southland, during the period when the abolition movement placed the institution of slavery on the defensive, abounds in similar arguments, in which slavery is justified as one of the ordinances of God. Not infrequently it is suggested in religious literature that it is the purpose of God to ordain poverty in order that the privileged may have a convenient opportunity for the exercise of their benevolent impulses, an argument which might well be kept from the eyes and ears of the poor themselves.

Another reason why a religiously inspired ethical sensitivity is more likely to create philanthropy than social justice, is that religion is constitutionally preoccupied with the motives of ethical actions and finds it difficult to deal with an entire social situation. Religion is more interested in the development of the spirit of love in the hearts of men, as a mark of personal perfection, than in love as an instrument of social redemption. The absurd suggestion that the poor afford the rich an occasion for the exercise of philanthropy is rather closer to the logic of religion than a sympathetic critic would like to admit. Religion is, on the whole, an affair of the will and the

[2]Quoted in B. K. Gray's *History of English Philanthropy,* p. 96.

emotions, rather than of the mind. At its best, it transfigures the will, giving the whole of man's character a
foundation in the will to do good. At its worst, it effects
only transient emotions and sinks very easily into sentimentality. Frequently it is only the man in dire distress,
and the situation which portrays social need in vivid
terms, that arouse the religious heart. Any social situation which requires careful analysis before moral responsibilities can be weighed and apportioned is much less
likely to appeal to the religious spirit or arouse the religious emotion. It is possible, of course, to wed a critical
and scientific intelligence to religious impulse, but the
union is not quite a natural one and is not often achieved.
The religious impulse, left to its own devices, expresses
itself in tenderness and sympathy whenever suitable
occasion presents itself, without asking too many questions about the consequences of this philanthropic
impulse or the comparative urgency of this particular
need in relation to other social needs.

In the letter of the Shepherd of Hermas, written in
the second century, a letter which had almost apostolic
authority in the early church, indiscriminate charity is
enjoined in the words "Give to all in simplicity without
asking to whom to give. Those who take without real
need must answer to God. But the giver is innocent in
any event."[3] Clement of Alexandria, in a similar spirit,
warns against discrimination in philanthropy, "For by
being fastidious and setting thyself to try who are fit for
thy benevolence, and who are not, it is possible that thou

---

[3]Quoted in G. Uhlhorn, *Christian Charity in the Ancient Church,* p. 121.

mayest neglect some who are friends of God."[4] The Didaché even suggests that the Christian should be impatient with his alms and press them, as it were, upon the first comer: "Let thine alms sweat in thine hand until thou know to whom to give them."[5] Every modern social worker has come into contact with a similar spirit in modern religious organizations and knows how difficult it sometimes is to restrain religious organizations, bent upon good deeds, until the merit of their project may be investigated and they may know whether or not their cause is worthy and its anticipated consequences salutary. The Catholic Church with its great institutional charities, offering a channel for the benevolent impulses which religion creates, is under less temptation in this respect than many Protestant congregations which, at Christmas, Thanksgiving, and other occasions when time and season prompt the benevolent impulse, bestow their charities upon whoever happens to be a convenient recipient. Except the religious benevolent impulse be guided by astute and intelligent leadership, it will not even ask what happens to the poor between the times when generous Thanksgiving and Christmas baskets are bestowed upon them.

In its purest form, religious benevolence is more than philanthropy. A highly sensitized religious spirit expresses itself as Christians expressed themselves in the apostolic church; they withheld nothing of their own from anyone in need, which means that they lived in a voluntaristic communism. Inevitably, however, this com-

---

[4]*Ibid.*, p. 121.
[5]Quoted by K. E. Kirk, *Vision of God,* p. 131.

plete mutuality degenerated into more conventional charity and almsgiving. It might have developed into a social organization in which carefully planned social strategy would have preserved the values of mutuality spontaneously achieved in the early intimate community. But that would have required thought and shrewd political calculation, and these are foreign to the religious spirit in its unspoiled form. There is a constitutional individualism in religion which derives from its reliance upon emotion and sentiment. It does not naturally concern itself with the political issues which arise when one tries to translate a moral ideal into terms relevant to the problems of an entire society. Religion does not deal with the problems of justice, for justice is a concept which emerges when a careful calculation is made of conflicting rights and competing responsibilities. Equalitarianism, which is the most rigorous type of justice, has never been born out of the heart of religion. It is a typical product of the mind. It is when intelligence discounts all the deceptions and hypocrisies by which inequalities of privilege are maintained and justified that the idea of equality, as a rational goal of social organization, emerges. Religion produces either more or less than that. At its best, it produces more, for it is willing to grant the neighbor what he needs without respect to competing needs. Unfortunately religion is not often maintained at that high level, and so it usually expresses itself in a charity which is less than justice.

The sentimentalities of charity are not, as already suggested, purely the product of the religious spirit. They spring from a natural limitation of the human mind and imagination. Many a secular philanthropist, who prides himself upon his benevolence, is unconsciously expressing his power in his benefactions, and would be stricken with horror if a just and intelligent society reduced his privileges to terms consonant with his service to society, depriving him of the luxury of feeling unselfish while he selfishly maintains most of his essential privileges. Radical proletarians are critical of benevolence and philanthropy of all kinds not only because they know it to be inadequate to their social needs, but also because they feel it to be a luxury beyond their reach, a luxury charged with hypocrisy which only those are able to indulge who have resources beyond their needs. Jesus judged very critically the benevolence of the rich who "gave of their superfluity," and his criticism is the natural reaction of a very pure religion which detects selfishness, even when it expresses itself in the subtlest forms. But since religion is only rarely upon that high plane of spiritual insight, it easily conspires with the inevitable hypocrisies of the privileged, who do not want justice, but who find satisfaction in expressing pity and power in the same act. In every act of philanthropy there is a temptation to think: "I am glad to help you, my poor man, as long as you recognize that I am the strong man and are duly grateful to me for my generosity in sharing my privileges with you, and do not raise too many impious questions about the sources and the justice of my privileges and your poverty."

Since the depression reached America, we have been treated to the hypocrisies which flow from voluntary charity, upon a national scale. America alone, of all industrial nations, has failed to learn the lesson that voluntary charity is insufficient to establish justice or to alleviate actual human suffering when society deals with a basic problem of distribution of wealth. Charity flows only where human need is vividly displayed and where it is recognized in intimate contact. Furthermore, charity, depending upon the emotions, is unreliable and unstable. Its impulses are not sustained. It can provide for the needs created by a sudden catastrophe or mitigate the miseries of those who are in dire and easily recognized distress. But it cannot do justice to social needs which arise out of the maladjustments of a mechanical civilization and are obscured amidst the impersonal relationships of an urban civilization. The effort to make voluntary charity solve the problems of a major social crisis, on the score that it represents a higher type of spirituality than coerced giving through taxation, results merely in monumental hypocrisies and tempts selfish people to regard themselves as unselfish. Every effort to judge social action merely by the purity of its motives, *i.e.*, the voluntary character, inevitably results in action which is less than sufficient for the social needs. The best proof of that is a comparison between our meager provisions for the unemployed and the more ample provisions of the poorer European nations which tax their citizens in order to provide adequately for those out of work.

While social conservatism, therefore, is not to be attributed only to religiously inspired philanthropy, but expresses itself as a by-product of all uncritical philanthropy, and as a product of the natural deceptions and illusions of uncritical minds, it is obvious that wherever religion places too high a premium upon spontaneity and follows its inclination to appreciate sentiment and to depreciate cool calculation, it plays into the hands of social conservatism and hypocritical sentimentality.

It would be well to note that, whatever the weaknesses of religion in this respect, there are always some strata in religious life where a more rigorous demand for social justice is made and in which religious perfectionism expresses itself not in ambition for a pure individual act of love, but in hopes for a perfect and just society. The eighth-century prophets of Israel had such hopes and, from the perspective of their ideal, they excoriated the rich who trampled upon the poor and "turned aside the needy at the gate," who "lay upon beds of ivory" and were indifferent to social injustice. In the medieval period, religious radicalism expressed itself chiefly in monasticism, which tried to make a clean break with the injustices of society by creating a fellowship of poverty and love within, and yet outside of, the social order. This type of radicalism did not try to change the order of society, but it did not, at least, accept it nor give it religious justification.

Since the Reformation, the main currents of Protestant thought have been middle class and conservative, but the radical tradition has been maintained by various sects and groups within the churches. Among the Diggers, the Levellers, the Brownists, and the early Quakers, religion expressed itself in a radical criticism of the injustices of society, a vigorous effort to establish social justice within the religious community—an effort which frequently resulted in communistic experiments of various kinds, and in an apocalyptic hope of the coming of a just society. It cannot be denied that most of these sects which elaborated radical social philosophies sprang from the lower and disinherited classes, and that their religious idealism was influenced by their economic interest, or at least by their own social experience. But frequently their radicalism outlasted their low estate. The Quakers for instance, even after they became prosperous or began to appeal to the more prosperous classes, maintained their opposition to class and caste, were in the forefront of the battle against slavery and war, and opposed luxurious living standards.

The attitude of the middle class churches to these radical religious programs was frequently inspired by a self-righteous feeling that poverty is due to vice and laziness and that social comfort is the inevitable reward of virtue. This kind of complacency may have been the natural attitude of middle class life with its individualism, its lack of social imagination, its blindness to the more profound social issues. It may have resulted naturally from the limited experience of the middle classes, who frequently rose from genteel poverty to genteel comfort by dint of their diligence and thrift. But since it clothed itself very frequently in the garments of religious piety, particularly in Calvinistic and Puritan religion, it must be mentioned as a social attitude which religion sometimes produces or justifies. In *The Art of Thriving,* published in the seventeenth century, the logic of this attitude is put thus forcibly:

Though complaints of poverty and scarcity of money are unhappily become no less general than lamentable, so that wherever we go our ears are assaulted with the sad rhetoric of beggary and our eyes with the deplorable objects of pity, yet it must be acknowledged that we rail impertinently at the hardness of the times since tis ourselves that make them such. Men generally by sloth and vanity, negligence and extravagance twist those chains of necessity wherein they lie entangled. Wherefore let everyone wipe his eyes and make use of his head and his hands to preserve or recover himself from the quagmire of want, it being certain that still every man in health and in strength may forge himself out a fortune by industry and frugality and obtain, (though not a splendid yet) a comfortable subsistence.[5]

With such a complacent attitude toward poverty and its problems, it was natural that middle class churches should give little sympathy to the more radical proposals of the sects. Gray declares:

The Anglican and Puritan divines were at issue upon almost every conceivable consideration of abstract thought and political theory but they were in agreement in their common hostility to anything in the nature of a social revolution. The bases of the civil order were not open to criticism.[6]

That remains on the whole the attitude of the middle class church today, in every country. The Christian church, particularly the Protestant Church, is predominantly middle class and the middle classes are more naïve in their social outlook and less mindful of the deeper problems of social reorganizations, not only than the disinherited, but than the more aristocratic classes. It is inevitable, therefore, that their institutions of religion should be tainted by their social conservatism and complacency, particularly since there is in conventional

[5]Quoted by B. K. Gray, *History of English Philanthropy*, p. 208.
[6]*Ibid.*, p. 76.

religion itself a tendency to regard poverty as a fruit of vice and prosperity as the reward of virtue. There are impulses in vital religion which are at war with this tendency, but it usually gains the ascendency in conventional religion. Religious philanthropy, therefore, continues to attempt the expression of generous impulses without raising ultimate questions about the causes of social maladjustments which create the necessity of charity.

III

RELIGION AS A SOURCE OF MENTAL
AND SOCIAL HEALTH

We may readily assume that three-fourths of our social workers in this country function under secular auspices. The percentage for case workers is probably even higher. Those who work under religious auspices are prompted, both by their own convictions and by the traditions of the organization to which they belong, to take cognizance of religion as a force in the lives of the people to whom they minister. The secular social workers are more inclined to disregard religion. Some of them, who have come in contact with the deleterious effects of certain types of religion are even hostile to it. In another chapter we shall consider the validity of this critical attitude toward religion. But a discriminating attitude toward the forces of religion which we find among those entrusted to us is of equal importance for all of us, lest we destroy or remain oblivious to resources which we might well use for the redemption of human life from chaos to order.

Religion is first of all a force of order and unity in the lives of individuals. Men differ from brutes, in that the impulses of their lives do not possess a natural and inevitable harmony and unity. There are dozens of different ways in which the forces with which we are endowed by nature may be integrated. The dynamics of life may be directed into many different channels, according as personal inclination and family and national tradition, prompt the choice of a dominant interest or sanction a particular type of behavior. Any one of many varying impulses may become the organizing center of a life, and the other impulses may be grouped around it in many patterns and configurations. The unity and order of a life depend upon the emotional power and the moral inclusiveness of that life's guiding principle. If the character of an individual be centered on a primary impulse, such as sex, for instance, the principle of unity may be powerful, but may lack the inclusiveness to bring order into life. If loyalty to the family be the unifying principle of life's impulses, the sex impulse will take its important, but subordinate, place among many others, though family loyalty may not be inclusive enough to give a satisfactory organization of life for all purposes. Ideally, religion is the commitment of life to the highest values, conceived as the will of God. The moral potency of Christ in the Christian religion is derived from the fact that he is to the religious imagination the symbol of the best that life can be. The individual who commits himself to Christ usually does not, and may never, fully understand the significance of all the ethical positions which are associated with the historical Jesus. Sometimes the symbol remains devoid of any specific moral meaning. It stands in general only for the good life, the specific meaning of which is given by the problems which the individual faces and the circumstances in which he stands.

and is at the same time inhibited from changing its *mores* because these are sanctified by religion. This very religion, may, however, be a wholesome force in the lives of individuals who, but for it, would become victims of life's anarchic impulses, with no force strong enough to direct the multifarious impulses of life into a central channel. Irwin Edman, in analyzing the chaos in which many modern individuals live, has wisely observed that a crazy pattern for life is better than no pattern at all.[2] It is a significant fact that the percentage of crime in our cities is much higher among children of immigrants than among immigrants themselves. The moral and religious traditions of the newcomers, usually formed in European peasant life, may be inadequate for the larger problems of an urban civilization, but they prevent the first generation, among whom they have not disintegrated, from making shipwreck of their individual lives. In the second generation, the "acids of modernity," the conflict of various competing cultures and religious traditions, and the disintegrating effect of urban life upon all religious and cultural traditions, emancipate the young people from any discipline powerful enough to order their lives. Oswald Spengler has made a convincing analysis of the decadence of culture and morals which inevitably results from the impersonal relationships of urban life, producing foot-loose and rootless individuals who fall into chaos because they are not integrally related to any great tradition.

It is always possible to a few individuals to live by a rational discipline, which borrows from various religious

[2]*The Contemporary and His Soul.*

traditions but is subject to none. It may be doubted whether such discipline ever produces the vitality characteristic of a high religious mandate, except when it, as T. S. Elliot suggests, lives parasitically upon the religious convictions of the past. But whatever may be possible for a small group of intellectuals, the masses of men need to have their lives ordered by religious convictions. Sometimes, as in the case of communism, the convictions are avowedly nonreligious, but the avowal does not make them so. As long as they transcend the bounds of rationality, as must all ultimate affirmations about what life is and ought to be, they are religious. Life itself it not rational. Reason may refine and qualify our central convictions and redirect and divert our central loyalties, but the loyalties themselves are religious because they spring from either primary or inherited conceptions of the meaning of life and the goal of existence, these invariably implying an ultrarational affirmation.

A very wise social worker of my acquaintance, himself quite irreligious, has always made it a practice, when dealing with problem boys, to strengthen their religious heritage. He has felt that this offered him a fulcrum which could not be replaced by any other force. The crime problem of American cities, which we try to solve by ever greater police vigilance, is really only a symptom of the spiritual chaos in which the average urbanite lives. It is more accentuated in American, than in European cities, because in Europe the city is still organically alive to a national religious and cultural inheritance, which does not exist for the sons and daughters of immigrants in our American cities. It is a question whether a mechan-

be the highest possible goal which the rational analysis of a particular moral problem would offer; on the other hand, it may on occasion be higher. It may suggest an altruism which prompts a giving of the self beyond anything that a cool and calculating reason would suggest.

Real religious conversion, if it follows the certainties and assurances implied in the Christian religion, contains another element of great therapeutic value, though this is an element which sophisticated people understand very little—the assurance of grace and forgiveness. Modern thought is too deterministic and too impressed with the sequence of cause and effect to have any great confidence in this assurance. It is particularly critical of it because religious grace has so frequently degenerated into magic. It must be admitted that even when this does not occur, even when the religious experience of grace and forgiveness is preserved as a personal mystical experience, it has its moral dangers. It easily hampers moral effort, and offers men a short cut to that peace which ought to come only to those who have made a valiant effort. Nevertheless, it rests upon experiences of life and satisfies necessities, much more real than the sophisticated modern can realize. The idea of the love of God, which forgives sins and gives us the assurance that "though your sins be as scarlet they shall be as white as snow," is not purely a figment of the imagination. It is the religious symbol for a real force which reveals itself in life, the healing force. Even in nature there are healing and redemptive forces. The tree struck by lightning need not always perish: the rent in its side may be covered and its bleeding stopped by nature's own forces. How could a great urban community exist without asphyxiating itself, were it not for a generous alchemy of nature which purifies the polluted air? In the sphere of human and moral relations, the love of those who are nearest and dearest to us and who do not lose confidence in us in spite of our weaknesses and failings, is, and has always been regarded by the religious imagination, as a symbol of the benevolence and the forgiving love of God. What religion does is to heighten and to give cosmic significance to the fact that there are healing and redemptive forces at work in life, and that Omar's mournful conclusion:

> The moving finger writes; and having writ,
> Moves on, nor all your piety nor all your wit
> Shall lure it back to cancel half a line
> Nor all your tears wash out a word of it,

is not really true. For all who have fallen into confusion and who have become the victims of circumstances and of their own passions, there is a tremendously helpful and therapeutic value in the assurance of religion that the past can be conquered and need not tyrannize over the present or the future. The social worker who does not understand the mysteries of life out of which this assurance is born, and who regards this whole aspect of the religious life as a relic of a superstitious past, will never be able to make the redemptive forces in religion fully available to those who are in need of them.

Religion may be a resource not only to those who suffer from inner confusion, but to those who have become the victims of untoward circumstances and who face the perils of an uncertain and an insecure existence.

There is a sense of security in religion. The religious person is able to cultivate an optimism, which, in its more decadent forms, creates romantic illusions about the goodness of life, with which the facts do not square but which in its purer and more classical aspect is simply a kind of heroic courage which appeals from the immediate to the ultimate in life. About the therapeutic value of this religious sense of security, it would be well to let a psychotherapist speak:

In this place I need only indicate the close connection between restfulness of mind, so essential to the cure of nervous ills, and that characteristic of religious devotion. "They that *wait* on the Lord shall *renew* their strength." There is the alternation of repose and work, and the insistence of the source of strength being of a psychical and not a physical character. Christianity also teaches that to learn to rest, not only in moments snatched from our work but by keeping a mind free from worry and anxiety, neither caring for the morrow nor fearful of the forgiven past, is to give ourselves the opportunity of drawing on that "ample re-supply" which comes to those who do not fear to expend their energy for others. Life will throb within and through us, but our souls will be in repose.

The religious writings of men of old constantly emphasized confidence and cheerfulness as the keynote to strength. "In quietness and confidence shall be your strength." "Let not your heart be troubled." "Be not anxious." "Be of good cheer, I have overcome the world." "Say unto them of a fearful heart, 'Be strong, fear not.'" Such words as the following are literally fulfilled before our eyes in a shell-shock hospital of the present day. "The eyes of the blind shall be opened, and the ears of the deaf be unstopped. Then shall the lame man leap as an hart and the tongue of the dumb shall sing. They shall obtain gladness and joy, and sorrow and sighing shall flee away." Accurately and wonderfully these words describe both the treatment by the suggestion of confidence and its effects, as well on the body as on the mind.

This power which the Church has lost is being rediscovered, but along different lines. The psychotherapist, who is a physician of the soul, has been compelled to acknowledge the validity of the practical principles of the Christian religion, though he may or may not accept the doctrines on which they are said to be based.

Speaking as a student of psychotherapy, who, as such, has no concern with theology, I am convinced that the Christian religion is one of the most valuable and potent influences that we possess for producing that harmony and peace of mind and that confidence of soul which is needed to bring health and power to a large proportion of nervous patients. In some cases I have attempted to cure nervous patients with suggestions of quietness and confidence, but without success until I have linked these suggestions on to that faith in the power of God which is the substance of the Christian's confidence and hope. Then the patient has become strong.[3]

The critic of religion will pounce upon this aspect of the religious life and make some rather telling charges against it. He will say that it propagates illusion and offers men the opportunity to escape from the real, into an imaginary world, that it perpetuates a childish sense of dependence and prevents men from reaching full emotional maturity; and that it tempts men to accept untoward conditions in social life with greater equanimity than is good for them. All these charges contain a measure of truth, but the religious sense of security is not so easily to be disposed of. There is illusion in religious optimism only if the hard facts of life are denied, and there is escape only if the difficulties of the moment are not met. In the face of history, with its evidences of the splendid heroism of men and women who have believed that "underneath are the everlasting arms," it would be foolish to maintain that confidence in the ultimate beneficence of life and the cosmos incapacitates men from dealing realistically with their immediate problems. It

[3] J. A. Hadfield. *The Psychology of Power,* pp. 50-52.

may give them the very serenity and poise which they require to deal with them adequately. Their very faith in the goodness of life may be self-validating by releasing within themselves and within other men energies which will make them more nearly equal to the tasks which confront them. Human resources are never of fixed quantity or potency, and what men are potentially is just as real as what they are at a given moment. The ultimate affirmation of religion about the goodness of God remains, of course, a hypothesis of faith which can never be proved to those who are preoccupied with the chaos and evil which life reveals; neither can it be disproved to those who have felt it validated in their own inner experience. That is the character of religious faith; it must remain ultrarational to the end, because it makes the world that is external to man revelant to his enterprise, an absurdity according to every canon of pure rationality, but an absurdity which has in it the root of ultimate wisdom, and which is perpetrated by many unconsciously, even while they disavow it.

The charge that the optimism and the sense of security of religion inhibit men from dealing realistically with, and resisting bravely, the social evils from which they suffer, is perhaps the most serious and most plausible indictment which can be brought against it. The fact is that the religious strategy of life is admirable for dealing with circumstances which are immutable, but not so admirable when conditions are mutable and wait upon the will of man to change them. It is a virtue to know how to bear adversity bravely and to know "how to be abased and how to abound"; but if adversity should be due, not to capricious circumstance or the blindness of nature, but to the stupidity of man and the injustice of society, the virtue of religion becomes dubious. The fact is that the religious approach is much better suited to cope with the problems of man in nature, than those of man in society; *i.e.*, it is more nearly adequate to the task of wresting victory from defeat in man's unequal struggle with the hostile forces of the natural world, than to the task of making human society habitable for the human spirit. The radicals who insist that religion is an opiate for the people are partly right; and they will never know that they are partly wrong until they have built their ideal society. Then they will discover that even there men will suffer from disease, face death, confront untoward fortune, and endure many indignities from a world which is partly beneficent, but also hostile to human enterprise. "Man," said Robert Louis Stevenson, "is not destined to succeed; failure is the fate allotted to all men." In the sense that this is true, religion will always have a word to say about the manner in which failure can be turned into victory; and it will be scorned by men only in those brief periods in which they imagine that all the ills of mankind can be eliminated by building a new social order. All this does not change the fact that in those particular periods of history when old societies are crumbling and new ones must be constructed, periods such as the one we are living in now, religion will frequently be a force of reaction, because the tranquility and security which it creates may transcend all vicissitudes of time and tempt men to an attitude of detachment from the historical and social problems which they ought to

in religious life, operate to mitigate the inevitable frictions which occur in community life. In all true religion there is a sense of humility and contrition which operates to destroy the natural moral conceit from which all men suffer, or to which all men are tempted. "Why," said Jesus, "beholdest thou the mote that is in thy brother's eye, and considerest not the beam that is in thine own eye?" [5] That insight which prompts to a more critical appraisal of the self and a more sympathetic appraisal of the neighbor, is a true and authentic attribute of high religion, and it reveals how naturally contrition and forgiveness are related to each other. We can deal lovingly with our brothers, only if we have discovered the analogues of their limitations in our own souls. Any searching analysis of human motives and human actions should make it possible for us to realize the common and universal roots of all human frailties; but the fact is that only religious insight provides a sufficiently rigorous analysis for this purpose. It alone looks at human nature from a perspective high enough to discover the insignificance in the differences in virtue and attainment between men, and to know that "in Thy sight no man living is justified."

The sanifying influence of the religious spirit in communal life is nowhere more apparent than in family life. Religion operates best in intimate communities, because the impulses of religion lose some of their virtue when they cannot find a direct and immediate application; they must be wedded to the astute social intelligence which is needed to guide the moral will through complex social

[5]Matthew 7:3.

relations. In the family, where relations are intimate but where points of friction are therefore correspondingly frequent, nature herself provides forces which soften these points of friction. Yet the natural attraction of sex is not always sufficient to prevent calamity in family life. Where religion encourages attitudes of mutual forbearance and forgiveness, and where it emphasizes the sacramental character of the family union, thereby assuming its permanence, an atmosphere is created in which difficulties are resolved much more easily than in a purely secular atmosphere. It might not be too strong an assertion to say that religion has achieved its highest triumphs in family life. While divorce is steadily increasing and is quite frequent among those who are nominally religious, it is an unchallenged fact that divorce is a very rare occurrence among families in which vital religion is maintained.

Social workers must deal increasingly with the problems of broken homes, and homes near the breaking point. It is not suggested that they can supply the religious resources where the unfortunate family is in need of them. But they can make use of whatever religious resource still exists in the family; and sometimes, if they realize how powerful this may be, they may be enabled to strengthen it sufficiently to make of it a redemptive force in the imperiled unity of the family.

IV

RELIGION AS A CAUSE OF PERSONAL
AND SOCIAL MALADJUSTMENT

When dealing with the influence of religion upon life, we must proceed upon the assumption of its transcendent importance, but not upon that of its invariable virtue. The conflicting estimates of the social and moral usefulness of religion, emanating from its devotees and its foes, are due not merely to contrasting biases, but to the fact that religion is actually, or may be, a deleterious, as well as a wholesome influence. Those personally biased in favor of, or in opposition to, religion are always able to select evidence in justification of their position. There is enough evidence on either side.

Religious faith unifies individuals, stabilizes societies, creates social imagination and sanifies social life; but it also perpetuates ancient evils, increases social inertia, creates illusions and preserves superstitions. It also accentuates introspection to the point of morbidity, and it frequently reduces moral sensitivity to the point of prurience. Social workers constantly come into contact with men and women who suffer from the inadequate types of religion, or from religious experiences and forces applied inopportunely or given undue emphasis. About religion, as about every high value of the life of man, the words of Shakespeare are true:

> The sweetest things turn sourest by their deeds,
> Lillies that fester smell far worse than weeds.

One fruitful cause of social maladjustment with which social workers come into frequent contact is the divisive character of religious loyalties in the family and in the community. Religion tends to absolutize everything which it touches. It places the sanctity of the divine and the eternal upon the social customs and the group relations to which it is organically related. Frequently it will do this, even when new social experience and conflicting social loyalties ought to be given preference by every right of reason. A common religion, as we have seen, may unify a home, but divergent religious traditions are frequently responsible for broken homes. There are many happy families in which the Catholic-Protestant or the Jew-Gentile chasm has been bridged. Where there is more than an ordinary measure of social grace and family affection, the possibilities of friction, arising from divergent religious loyalties, may be overcome. But this is not always done. In family life, every common interest and every common loyalty is a gain, and every divisive influence is a hazard. Father Moore, in his *Dynamic Psychology*, gives an illustration of a more than ordinarily serious consequence of religious friction in the family:

Thus, in one instance, a woman was having periodic convulsive seizures of an hysterical character for which the best specialists that she had consulted could find no cause. The mental history of the patient revealed the fact that she had made an agreement with her husband before marriage that all the boys would be brought up Protestant, and the girls Catholic. This arrangement had been made subsequent to a prior one before the priest in which the usual promise had been made that all children would be brought up Catholic. After that the marriage was postponed, but she was later married, ostensibly on the basis of the first agreement, the

village they are an unmitigated evil. So much has been written upon this point that it is unnecessary to enlarge upon it here. More serious than the waste and division of responsibility which results from this denominationalism, is the actual social conflict which is frequently caused by religion. The religious issue is a potential cause of distraction in the political life of most of our urban communities, and the sudden recrudescence of the Ku Klux Klan in post-war years revealed how much religious prejudice still remains as a source of social friction in our American life. The Klan was in reality not an instrument of religious loyalty, but an expression of Nordic fears and hatreds against Negroes, Jews and south European immigrants. It was an expression of racial bigotry, rather than of religious prejudice, but the fact that it could hide its racial animosities behind religious loyalties gives us an interesting lesson in the uses to which religion may be put. It was the Nordic, rather than the Protestant, who expressed himself in the Klan; but, since the Nordic is also predominantly Protestant, he could indulge and create the illusion that loyalty to a Protestant heritage prompted his bigotries. Religion, as we have previously observed, always tends to give the relativities of time and place an absolute value in the eyes of the religious devotee. It adds a demoniac quality to the animosities derived from racial and political diversities, because of its touch of absolutism. The conflict between northern and southern Ireland is really a conflict between Irishmen and Scotchmen, but the fact that the Scotch are Protestant, and the Irish, Catholic, adds acrimony to the conflict because it gives each side the feeling that, while defending its own heritage, it is defending some absolute value which transcends its own racial or national life. Religion is always placing the counsels of an eternal God behind the limited insights, the partial perspectives and the circumscribed loyalties of the immediate moment.

This same *penchant* of religion is the root of another fruitful source of social maladjustment. Religion perpetuates family and community *mores* when new social experience counsels their amendment or abrogation. In Polish immigrant families, for instance, an autocratic family life, which exacts the wages of the children for the parents and allows the interference of the parents in the marital life of the children, is frequently maintained by religious authority, in the teeth of opposition prompted by freer American family traditions. In the same way, religious opposition to birth control frequently binds upon mothers burdens too grievous to be borne. In my personal experience, I have found more social workers impatient and critical of authoritarian religion, because of experiences dealing with this problem, than with any other. Hoping to relieve mothers of the burden of a child a year, they have been frustrated in their effort to make prenatal clinics available for these mothers by the interposition of religious authority. The church declares birth-control to be an interference with the "laws of nature," though it illogically enjoins celibacy upon the priesthood and thereby supplants the laws of nature in another way. Andrew White reports that in the nineteenth century the Scotch clergy opposed the use of an anesthetic in childbirth as being an "impious attempt to circumvent God's primeval curse upon women." That is a good illustration of the danger of religious sanctions, operating in complete irrelevance to the facts of experience and the needs of men.

Religious opposition to divorce, when maintained uncompromisingly, as in the Catholic Church, may easily result in intolerable conditions and unescapable indignities for a partner of a drunken or dissolute mate. The religious ideal of marriage as a sacrament has its own legitimacy as we have seen; but when an ideal is reduced to a law and enjoined upon those who lack the spiritual resources to achieve it, it may become a grievous burden. One might well believe that marriage ought to be permanent, if at all possible, without condoning the cruelties which men and women suffer because the permanency of marriage is made an absolute and unqualified law, for which exceptions are granted only in the rarest instances. Case workers who deal with family problems have again and again confronted religious intransigeance at this point, and have been tempted to curse the authority which religion still maintains in modern life.

Dozens of other examples could be presented to illustrate the social danger of religious authoritarianism, frequently perpetuating customs and *mores* which have little relevance to contemporary social experience and necessity, and which on occasion are positively perilous to the good life.

Frequently religious attitudes are characterized by a hard and unimaginative moralism which operates to aggravate the social and personal problems which social workers face. While a high type of religion insists on the mutuality of guilt in all situations, and while Jesus reproved those who wished to stone an erring woman by suggesting that the sinless one cast the first stone, yet the type of religion which suggested the stoning of the woman is probably more frequent than that which condemned this hardness of heart. Social workers are frequently called upon to deal with the problem of forbidding and unforgiving parents of unmarried mothers or wayward girls, these parents hiding a wounded family pride behind their pretensions of outraged family virtue. Their own share in the guilt of their offspring, frequently quite apparent to the unbiased observer, is of course not recognized by them. This kind of forbidding and unimaginative moralism is not necessarily the product of religion, and it may on occasion reveal itself among quite irreligious people; nevertheless, it has been particularly common among the conventionally religious. Conventional piety frequently accentuates self-righteousness and censoriousness.

Conventional religion, particularly if it represents a decadent Puritanism, frequently expresses an excessive and unbalanced moralism, not only in its unforgiving attitude toward the wayward, but in its unimaginative devotion to narrow and socially meaningless or harmless moral codes. Sabbath observance has been, on the whole, a blessing to the world, but there are still religious moralists who would rob workers of their one opportunity in the week for recreation by besetting the day with meaningless taboos against wholesome recreation. Prohibitions against theater going, card playing, and dancing may have more cultural than moral significance, though in regard to dancing, church prohibitions against a form of social intercourse which has grown practically universal, inhibits the church from entering into the full life of its young people, and encourages hypocrisy among them. The problems of sex have been dealt with helpfully by the church, only in periods when extreme laxity in sex relations made an uncompromising reaction to loose sex habits salutary. In other periods, only a few religious leaders and teachers have been able to rid themselves of a very old assumption that sex is impure, and of a corresponding prurience when dealing with matters of sex among young people. The Catholic Church has been saved from some of the worst evils in this respect by a dualistic ethic which permitted the church itself to be rather wise and shrewd in dealing with matters of sex, while the monastic movement directed the tendency of religion to regard sex as unclean into the particular channel of total abstinence—celibacy and virginity.

The attitude of religion toward sex, in which the modern moralists detect a lack both of balance and of shrewd understanding of the complexities of human nature, is typical of a very general limitation of religiously inspired morality, its fanaticism. Religion may create insights of its own, and it may result in imaginative perspectives of social relations and responsibilities, which derive directly from the religious dogma of a God-governed world or the religious experience of moral responsibility to God; but on many occasions religion only sharpens previous moral convictions and accentuates previously held moral attitudes. It is this note of extravagance in religion, particularly in vital religion, which prompted the Earl of

Roscommon to declare, "For one who is inspired ten thousand are possessed." The rational moralist arrives at his judgments by a careful analysis of all the values which are involved in a proposed action, and by an equally careful comparison of the relative claims of various values upon the agent. The virtues of a rational morality are therefore sober-mindedness and balance. Religion, on the other hand, is an affair of the emotions, or of ossified emotions embodied in tradition. In either case, it always involves a potential danger to a balanced view of a moral problem. If it is a sublime emotion that animates the religious devotee, his actions may achieve a nobility which the rationalist can never compass. Religion is madness, and it may be noble madness. But emotion may disturb the cool judgment which is as necessary to a high morality as to any other high value. It may lead to extravagances which emphasize one value involved in an action, as against all other values. If religion supports the prohibition movement, for instance, it is immediately tempted to disregard every other problem which may be involved with prohibition in a political struggle. Where a moral duty is simple but difficult, religious impulse is required to furnish the necessary dynamic for its fulfillment. But whenever a moral problem involves a complex situation with many conflicting and competing values, religion is usually not a helpful ally in the moral struggle. It oversimplifies the problem. If, as is frequently the case, religion should incorporate not a contemporary emotion, but a historical one, now embodied in a tradition, it will add irrelevance to fanaticism in its moral counsels.

The peril of rational morality is dilettantism; the same reason which directs the impulse to its goal, destroys the impulsive power. Men of reason may consolidate the gains of a previously creative period, and they may amend its minor limitations. But the gains are made by men of religion, in whose spirit the impulses of the flesh are fused with the impulse toward the ideal. Reason controls impulse, but religion transfigures it. Reason is never as creative and never as dangerous as religion. Religion is dangerous, both in its life and in its living death— tradition. It is dangerous in its life because its creative and vital impulses, impatient with the balancing force of reason, may give themselves to narrow ends; or they may give themselves to high ends but pay too great a price for their achievement. When the vital impulse of religion has become atrophied into a tradition, it may still order life and preserve unity within life's turbulent passions, but it is too blind to recognize the new forces which emerge in life and the new situations which the conscience faces. There is no final choice between reason and religion. There are too many virtues and too many vices in the camp of each. The good rationalist acts after analyzing all the factors which are involved in his action; the bad rationalist does not act at all, because he lacks the "inhibition quelling fury" which is supplied by religion and which would overwhelm all the scruples which his analysis had called forth. Good religion has intuitions which fuse all the finer impulses of life and unite them toward a high goal, without a too-careful analysis after the manner of the rationalists. Bad religion disturbs the balance of life and obsesses the soul with some absurd fancy or some moral end which is irrelevant to the real enterprise of a good life.

Unfortunately, we are living in a period of religious decay in which there is more secondary than primary religion. "When religion has become an orthodoxy," declared William James, "its day of inwardness is over; the spring is dry and the faithful live at second hand exclusively and stone the prophets in their turn," [2] The Catholic Church maintains *mores* which may have had meaning in the agrarian life of an Italian village a century ago, but which have little relevance to our society. The Protestant Church, except for a small sophisticated minority in the larger cities, who have absorbed modern culture almost to the point of losing their original religious heritage, lives by the standards of a Puritanism which had meaning for the middle classes of two centuries ago, when they asserted their morality of thrift and continence against the luxurious habits of the rich and the vulgarities and sensualities of the poor, but which has little meaning today amidst the complexities of an urban and industrial civilization. If we want to see the power of religion functioning creatively, with all the furor and all the fervor which characterize vital religion, with all the peril of fanaticism which belongs to anything creative, we have to turn to a sect which is most vociferous in disavowing religion, the communists. Communism may not be the highest possible type of religion, but it is worth studying because it is a religion which has vitality in our own day, and is not under the necessity of harking back to the past for its heroes and rebels. Its defects, its cruel-

[2] In *Varieties of Religious Experience.*

ties, and its blindness to some of the more ultimate problems of the human spirit are rather natural expressions of the limitations of modern man, bedeviled by an industrial civilization. But some of its limtiations are simply the limitations of religion *per se*. It is fanatic. It has one goal, an equalitarian ideal for society, and everything else is sacrificed for that goal. It, like all religion, is constantly saying, "This one thing I do." That is what ought to be said if we have found the one thing worth doing. But alas! it is so difficult to know if, and when, we have.

V

RELIGION AS A RESOURCE FOR THE SOCIAL WORKER

We have analyzed religion, both as a resource and as a complication in the lives of the people with whom the social worker deals. Let us look at it now as a resource for the social worker himself. If I understand the average modern social worker, he is very often of the type in whom traditional religion no longer awakens interest, who is affronted by the intellectual obscurantism in which conventional orthodoxy is clothed, or perplexed by the intellectual problems which the religious world view faces in our modern scientific culture; but he is probably engaged in social work precisely because that vocation is to him the most logical means of expressing his sense of mission to mankind, which has been aroused by the religion of his youth. I wonder how many social workers in America once dreamed in their youth of being missionaries. If the number who have confessed some similar ambition to me is any criterion, I should draw the conclusion that the army of American social workers are ex-ministers, if, for the moment, we give historic reality to the ambitions and vocational choices of youth. Many have found in their ministrations to the needy a practical substitute, not only for the types of social ministry traditionally associated with religious vocations, but for the more specificially religious disciplines and practices. A life of practical helpfulness to needy men gives them, they think, more solid satisfactions than is afforded in the vague and not generally applied idealisms of religious devotees.

The question is, whether the problems which they face can be solved with the highest degree of success, purely by the resources naturally created in the process of meeting and solving these problems. No wise person would deny that there is a great deal of wholesome, vital religion and spirituality which has nothing to do with traditional religious forms or customs, but which arises naturally from an imaginative relationship to the needs of men and an honest effort to meet these needs. But that does not exclude the possibility of living even more vitally and facing perplexing problems with even greater wisdom and fortitude, if the resources of religion are more consciously sought and appropriated. Religion is a sentiment, a conviction, and an attitude; but it is also a discipline, elaborated, perfected, corrupted, and rejuvenated by ages which have preceded us. We can subject ourselves to this discipline, test the hypotheses and assumptions upon which the discipline rests, cultivate the attitudes which it encourages, and associate ourselves with the noble spirits, living and dead, in whose lives historic religion is incarnate.

A vocation such as social work, in which the factor of personal human relations is particularly important, demands nothing so much as a sympathetic and imaginative approach to human beings. Human beings are such complexes of virtue and vice, of foibles which test our patience and nobilities which compel our admiration, that both the lovers of men and the misanthropes can find ample evidence for their particular bias in practically every member of the human race. Human contacts yield conclusions in regard to human nature, according to the assumptions with which they are initiated. We can love or hate men according as we will to love or hate them. Usually the will to love is prompted by consanguinity. We do not love, in other words, except as nature prompts the spirit. Within the family, except in cases where love meets actual malevolence, the spirit of love prevails, discovering and creating the stuff of character which justifies its assumption. Classical religion, as in the case of Jesus and those who have entered fully into his spirit, projects the attitudes which prevail in the family into the world. The whole human family lives under the fatherhood of God, and all men are brothers. The strong are to bear the burdens of the weak, and "in Christ there is to be neither Jew nor Gentile, neither bond nor free." The eye of religious imagination detects similarities, where the obvious view is obsessed by the differences created by circumstance and climate; and it sees potentialities where the secular view recognizes only immediate realities. Religion attempts to transcend and to transmute nature by extending the attitudes which prevail in the kinship group so as to include more than that immediate sib. "If ye love those who love ye," said Jesus, "what thanks have ye." The assumption upon which religion proceeds is not scientific. All men are not brothers. They are, in fact, continually arrayed in warring camps, and they are frequently enemies rather than brothers. But potentially they are brothers, and to assume that they are, will help to make them so. There is, of course, always the possibility that the religious imagination will lose touch with present realities and degenerate into sentimentality. Dealing with the difficult problem of inter-group relations, it frequently finds the establishment of brotherly relations too difficult and contents itself with veiling and obscuring the indecent and brutal facts of conflict by claiming reality for an ideal which has not been realized. Here religion faces a constitutional difficulty. It inculcates attitudes of trust and good will which operate with practically unvarying success in individual relationships, even if those relationships transcend the boundaries of class and race. But human groups are less trustworthy in their corporate actions than the individuals which compose them, and the religious approach to inter-group problems, particularly in the field of economics and politics, is therefore particularly subject to the corruption of sentimentality. Religious idealism finds tremendous difficulties in making itself effective in the economic and political life of our day. It usually makes a romantic analysis of the factors involved in a political problem. But about this we shall have more to say in the final chapter. These difficulties of religion, in the field of politics, cannot detract from the long history of triumphs which it is able to record in the field of personal human relations, where attitudes of trust and sympathy may have a direct influence upon the human object of these attitudes. Every human being carries within him potentialities and possibilities which will flower only under the warmth of love, unknown capacities which answer only to the call of trust.

Social workers are called upon to deal especially with the subnormal and the defective, the men and the women who have been brought low by their own limitations, though they must deal with an even greater number who have been victimized by untoward fortune. In the case of the former, a religiously inspired and sustained sympathy is frequently the only force which will overcome the temptation to contempt or loathing. A Francis of Assisi among the outcasts, a Father Damien among the lepers, an Albert Schweitzer among the careless children of the primeval forests of Africa, a John Howard among the prisoners of England, a Catholic nun among the Magdalenes of the street, these all bear witness to the power of religion to find the "child of God" in what the world condemns, rejects or despises. It must be admitted that religion is not itself able to provide the detailed knowledge of human motives and of the intricacies of human personality which is necessary to the most helpful treatment of maladjusted individuals. Religion, except in cases where it is expressed through highly gifted individuals who have an intuitive understanding of human character, does not supply what must be derived from the science of psychotherapy. The insights of religion are direct and immediate, but they are frequently impatient, too impatient, with detail. Nor is religion always as ready as it ought to be, to borrow resources from science. But it is not impossible to unite the insights of religion of a high type with the knowledge which science imparts.

Modern religion has frequently discredited the religious emphasis upon love and the religious appreciation of personality as having transcendent worth, by a sentimentality which derives much more from the romantic movement than from classical religion itself. For in classical religion there is always a paradoxical attitude toward human nature. Man is both a child of God and a sinner. The same God who loves man also convicts him of sin. For in the insight of true religion, God is not only loving but holy. He is not only the companion of man's way, but the goal toward which he is striving. In comparison with his holiness, man falls short and feels himself "an unprofitable servant." He regards "all his righteousnesses as filthy rags." There is always the suggestion that man ought to love his brethren not because they are, in the sight of God, as good as he, but because they are no worse. "All have fallen short of the glory of God." True religion produces not only love, but humility; and the love is partly a derivative of the spirit of contrition. We must forgive those who have wronged us, because we know the same evil to be in us. If we are not without sin, we cannot cast the contumelious stone.

This emphasis upon the sinfulness of man has been just as strong, in classical religion, as the emphasis upon his Godlikeness. It has saved religion, at its best, from the sentimentality into which modern culture has fallen since the romantic period, with its reaction to the dogma of man's total depravity by its absurd insistence upon the natural goodness of man. The real religious spirit has no illusions about human nature. It knows the heart of man to be sinful. It is therefore not subject to the cynical disillusion into which sentimentality degenerates when it comes into contact with the disappointing facts of human history.

The Rousseauist [declares Irving Babbitt][1] begins by walking through the world as though it were an enchanted garden, and then with the inevitable clash between his ideal and the real, he becomes morose and embittered. Since men have turned out not to be indiscriminately good, he inclines to look upon them as indiscriminately bad. . . . At the bottom of much so-called realism there is a special type of satire, a satire which is the product of violent emotional disillusion.

It is tremendously difficult, without the paradoxes of religion, to escape estimates of human nature which betray into absurdity by their consistency. Man is either good or bad, life is either sublime or not worth living, the universe is either man's friend or his enemy, according to the philosophies. In the insights of the Christian religion and in the poetic symbolism of all true religion, man is first driven to despair by the knowledge of his sins and then encouraged by the hope that redemption is possible for him. He finds life tragic but also worth living, because he beholds the beauty in the tragedy. In the universe he discovers both God and the devil, both friendly and unfriendly forces. The same God whom the religious devotee worships as omnipotent is not sufficiently powerful to overcome the devil, except in "the last days." There is always a note of absurdity in these paradoxes of religion, but the wise man will choose them in preference to the absurdities into which he is betrayed by the emphasis on the logical consistency of rational thought.

The belief that human beings are worthy of love because they are children of God, can be saved from sentimentality only by the shrewder insights of religion. The most sentimental religion of our day is, significantly, the

[1] *Rousseau and Romanticism,* p. 105.

type of liberal Christianity which has been most strongly influenced by the nineteenth century culture to which our generation still adheres. For an effective religious paradoxical attitude toward human nature, one must turn either to more orthodox religion or to the most contemporary of all religions, communism, which begins with the most cynical analysis of the selfishness of human life and ends with the most roseate hopes for the possibilities of human social coöperation, once men have been "redeemed" from a thwarting social system. Whatever fallacies may lurk in both the pessimism and the optimism of either classical or proletarian religion, they provide a basis for social attitudes which are realistic without cynicism, and trusting without degenerating into sentimentality.

The social worker needs the insights of religion, not only to keep wholesome his attitudes towards individuals for whom he is responsible, but also to preserve sanity and health in his outlook upon life and his particular mission therein. Without some kind of religion, it is not possible either to be assured of the significance of your mission or to be confident of the whole moral enterprise of which you feel it to be a part. A sense of vocation, if it is at all powerful, is always in some sense religious, though it may, of course, exist without conscious relationship to any traditional religion. The reason it must be religious is that it is impossible in terms of pure reason to choose a goal for your life and to believe in its importance. It is possible to make a rational comparison of competing objectives. I can determine by rational analysis that one type of vocation will contribute more directly to

the cause of social justice than another. I can also determine that social justice is a goal toward which all men
ought to strive. But I cannot, by reason, determine that
it is the goal. Reason is, in the last analysis, morally neu-
tral. If it is supported by some moral standard, it is able
to use such a criterion to determine the relation of various
lesser values to the supreme value, and to prompt the
choice of the most effective means to reach the desired
end. But our ultimate moral preference is not rational at
all. Reason can operate only after certain ultrarational
presuppositions have been made. We can believe, for
instance, that our mission in life must be to help all people
to gain fullness of life, and we can live under the illusion
that this is a rational moral goal. But this conviction is
impossible, if we have not first of all assumed that life
itself has a value. Nor can we define what we mean by
fullness without resorting to presuppositions which have
their roots in religion. The first assumption that life has
a value is so generally made that its religious character is
not usually recognized. But it is quite obvious that religion greatly influences the degree of enthusiasm which
men are able to express for the worth of life. Without a
religious assumption about life, it is not easy to escape
the conclusion that all is vanity. The will to live and the
will to live nobly are both irrational, the one subrational
and the other ultrarational. If we should decide that a
noble life means an unselfish life, that too will rest upon
a religious assumption. Reason is able, within limits, to
enjoin unselfishness, because it is possible to prove that
consistent selfishness is self-defeating. But it is not possible to prove rationally that we ought to attempt to gain

fullness of life for all men. We could, with George Jean Nathan, and many cynics before him, believe that most men are not worth the solicitude which we bestow upon them, and we could also believe that an aristocracy which rests upon social injustice creates certain cultural values impossible in an equalitarian democracy, and that these values are to be preferred to any which a democracy is able to bring forth. Our ultimate moral preferences, are, in short, ultrarational. They need not in every case be consciously religious, and they are frequently accepted so uncritically and are so thoroughly a part of the world view which we share with the group in which we live, that their rationality is taken for granted. But if they are traced back, they are always found ultimately to be derived from a total view of what life is and ought to be, which is religious. Sometimes unconscious religion is sufficient to maintain our sense of mission in life. But conscious religious discipline undoubtedly enhances tremendously the enthusiasm with which we are able to follow our vocation. Max Weber, the great German sociologist of religion, believes that modern business enterprise would have been impossible if Protestantism had not given the modern business man a religious sense of mission, and destroyed the inferiority complex under which he labored in the classical and medieval world. This very illustration reveals how dangerous the religious sense of mission may be. Cortéz and the Spanish conquerors were nerved to almost impossible feats of heroism and brutality by their religious sense of mission to Spain and to the Catholic Church. Religious assumptions are usually too emotional to allow themselves to be critically analyzed. That is at once their virtue and their vice. For the same critical analysis which may refine moral impulses and make moral preferences more discriminating, may destroy them completely. Mr. Joseph Wood Krutch has shown us in his book, *The Modern Temper,* how well that can be done.

Any vocation which defies the commercial traditions of our age and which dispenses with the concrete and immediate rewards which have become the badge of success in our day, is in particular need of religious support. In as far as social work is well paid, it may of course be prompted by a commercial motive. In every profession there is a conflict between the commercial and the vocational motives, the former strengthened by the fact that professional work is not poorly rewarded, if rewards are judged from the perspective of an absolute equalitarian standard, and the latter obviously operative as long as the concrete rewards fall below the measure which similar ability is able to command in commercial pursuits. The fact that genuine religion still prompts so many to enter social work in religious organizations in which financial rewards are absolutely at a minimum or, as in the case of the Catholic orders, nonexistent, proves how powerful religion is in strengthening the vocational, against the commercial, motive in life. To help those who are in need is an ambition which is prompted by the most natural of all human impulses, sympathy. But only when natural sympathy is reinforced by a religious belief that the ultimate value in life is love, can the emotion of sympathy, which like all emotions is unstable and transient, be made the basis of a vocation.

The social worker faces the temptation not only to regard his work as unimportant and insignificant, but to think of it as futile. Religious impulses may prompt him to believe that one ought to help the needy, but that is not enough. He will be assailed by the temptations of pessimism and despair. The ocean of human misery is so great that he will feel as if he were childishly draining it with a cup. This sense of futility is not altogether unwholesome, and ought not to be overcome too quickly by religious faith before it has led to a re-analysis of the objectives of social work and an examination of the effectiveness of traditional methods of achieving the ends of social justice. Nevertheless, even the most nearly perfect social strategy faces such insurmountable obstacles, sees so many new social problems arising for every problem solved, and finds the human stupidity and brutality, which create social need, given off from such vast reservoirs of human incompetence, that the intelligent worker will always be prone to despair.

Moral sensitivity inevitably leads to pessimism. Only callous men can be consistent optimists. Social intelligence likewise leads to pessimism. Only ignorant men are optimists. The sensitive man recognizes the extent of human misery, and the intelligent man knows how many hopes for a world in which injustice and human brutality would be eliminated, have been disappointed. He knows what a terrible inertia frustrates, or seems to frustrate, every redemptive and creative effort. He knows how frequently the conscious elimination of one social evil has been followed by the unconscious substitution of another. He sees human society conquering one social complexity, only to have an engineering advance create a new one. Human society seems to be fighting a losing battle, or rather, to be running a losing race, with its own technical apparatus, which always works for inhumanity because it requires such a long time before it can be subordinated to human ends.

Consideration of these facts may well prompt the social worker to consider whether modern society does not need a more thorough reorganization than most social workers envisage, and whether there is not actual futility in much that passes for social work. On that problem, I shall enlarge in my final chapter. Here it must be noted that even the most perfect social strategy has an element of seeming futility, when viewed from an absolute perspective. Nothing that is worth doing seems ever possible of accomplishment. Certainly nothing that is worth doing can ever be completed in the life of one generation. Every Moses perishes outside of the promised land and can behold it only through the eyes of faith. Religion is the hope that grows out of despair. It is the ultimate optimism which follows in the wake of a thorough pessimism. One reason why our generation is not religious is that it has been too sentimental to be thoroughly pessimistic. It has never looked into the bottomless abyss, on the edge of which all the citadels of faith are built. Any easy optimism, such as the nineteenth century's idea of progress and the evolutionary optimism of the early twentieth century, is both the cause and the consequence of a deterioration of religious feeling. If progress be regarded as automatic, there is no real place for religion, however

diligent may be the effort to read God into the evolutionary process.

Religious optimism, the feeling that, in spite of everything, good will conquer and virtue will prevail, that the
universe has a moral basis, whatever the immediate evidences to the contrary, and that human enterprise is not
destined to futility, is partly the inevitable by-product of
strenuous moral energy. Pure pessimism is a bitter-sweet
luxury in which those indulge who prefer to observe the
scene of history, rather than to live in it, just as pure
optimism characterizes the ignorant, the naïve, and the
dilettante. Those who act with both circumspection and
energy, create their own religious emotion. No real revo-
lutionist doubts that the revolution will prevail and that
it will usher an ideal social order into being. Every real
prophet dreams of the day when the lion will lie down
with the lamb. Every true religion has its millennial
hope, which will seem foolishness to the wise, but to
"those who are called, the power of God and the wisdom
of God." The optimism of traditional religion is but the
stereotyped and conventionalized form of the optimism
which was created in some morally energetic period of
religion, upon which the subsequent generations feed.
The priest dispenses the certainties and the hopes which
the prophet created. It may seem that this process of
stereotyping optimism and making it available for those
who have failed to create it by their own energy,
increases the element of illusion which is an inevitable
by-product of religious hope. Nevertheless, there are
certain advantages in this development. The average
man does not live so dynamically, and the springs of life

do not flow so purely in him, that he is able to maintain a wholesome attitude toward life without leaning a little on spiritual resources created by other more dynamic and more vigorous persons. If this attempt to borrow strength from others, which is the very basis of all institutional religion, does not tempt us to cease from all effort of our own, it can be a source of real moral power. Though the hopes of religion always have an element of illusion (the Resurrection is significantly not so well attested historically as the Crucifixion) there is good reason to believe that the world views, which come from the insights of morally and spiritually energetic men, are as true, and more potent, than the philosophies of mere observers. To live by the faith of religion means, then, that we will take our guidance from those who have lived most heroically; but we will remember that historical heroism alone will not preserve our optimism if we cannot contribute some genuine heroism of our own. "If," said the apostle Paul, "ye will not die with him, neither can ye reign with him."

VI

RELIGION AND SOCIAL ACTION IN MODERN LIFE

The most significant characteristic of modern life, from the perspective of the spiritual and social needs of modern men, is the technological nature of our civilization. Modern means of production and communication have created a society in which millions of men are brought into terms of economic interdependence without having any necessary organic relationship or sense of moral and spiritual fellowship. The modern factory unites thousands of workers in a common enterprise, but there is nothing in the processes in which they are engaged which relates them personally to one another. If they achieve some kind of moral unity through their own organizations and unions, it must frequently be done in defiance of the factory ownership. The "production belt," which tyrannically synchronizes the labor of hundreds, creates no spiritual bond between them. The modern city is as impersonal and mechanical as the factory. Means of rapid transit have made it possible for more and more people to congregate in urban centers, in which they live with only a minimum sense of social responsibility, since their civic relations are not sufficiently personal, and the actual machinery of government is too remote, to arouse their sense of communal responsibility. The same means of production and transit relate these people—who are

unable to develop sufficient civic responsibility to preserve sanity and decency in their urban life—to the whole
world, in terms of intimate economic interdependence,
without endowing them with the social intelligence which
makes such intimate relations sufferable. The modern
machine has, in short, made neighbors strangers, and
strangers neighbors. We do not know those who live
near to us, and we are dependent upon those who are far
from us.

Furthermore, the same means of production and communication which have increased the extent and intensity
of social cohesion, have centralized economic and social
power. All essential power in our modern society is economic power, the power of ownership. Economic power
is always able to bend political power to its own uses.
Economic power has always been extremely formidable,
but in modern society it has risen to greater heights and
become the source of more injustice than in any other,
because the private ownership of the productive processes
and the increased centralization of the resultant power in
the hands of a few, make inevitably for irresponsibility.
The cynic might easily interpret the history of mankind
as the history of the human brotherhood's losing struggle
with civilization, each new complexity adding to the difficulty of maintaining brotherly relations among human
beings. An agrarian civilization was in many respects less
ethical than a nomadic one, as the strictures of the
eighth-century Hebrew prophets, against the iniquities
of a settled civilization, made in the name of ideals
of brotherhood gained in the nomadic period, offer interesting evidence. Commercial civilizations tended to

increase the social injustices which began with the dispar-
ity of power created in agrarian civilizations by private
ownership; and industrial civilization has further heightened the social injustice which followed inevitably the
centralization of power. Human nature is neither purely
selfish nor purely unselfish. The possession of power,
whether economic, political, or military, tends to increase
both the extent and the destructiveness of human selfishness, because it defies the forces of self-restraint and
social restraint which have been built up against the
expression of such selfishness.

Modern man is, for these reasons, faced with tremendous social and moral problems. The impersonal relations of an urban, industrial civilization discourage the
expression of ordinary human sympathy, the basis of all
moral action. The mechanical character of urban and
industrial life tends to destroy moral and cultural traditions which developed in more organic types of society,
and makes the emergence of new cultural traditions
extremely difficult. Individual character, therefore,
comes under the peril of undisciplined impulses; and
vice and crime add their quota to the injustices which
urban life has multiplied. The complexity of modern
life, furthermore, demands a degree of social intelligence which does not flow naturally from the moral
impulses still existing in our day, so that, even when
moral good will is still operative, it does not insure moral
action. It is not surprising that, in such a civilization,
with personal discipline weakened, with social responsibility destroyed, with economic relations robbed of their
personal character, and with economic power increased

without any sense of responsibility for their fellowmen. A proper social pedagogy could probably accomplish even more than has been accomplished in the matter of bringing social responsibility to the consciousness of apartment-house dwellers and suburbanites who, unless some educational pressure were brought to bear upon them, would lose all sense of organic relation to the needy of their city. It must be admitted, of course, that even the most effective social pedagogy does not eliminate the moral hazard of impersonal relations in urban life, and it never provides more than a thin trickle of philanthropic finance, totally inadequate for the real needs of the people. This means that there are social problems in modern society which can be solved only in political terms. The fact that social workers so frequently fail to think beyond the present social and economic system, and confine their activities to the task of making human relations more sufferable within terms of an unjust social order, places them in the same category as the religious philanthropists whose lack of imagination in this respect we have previously deplored. A great deal of social effort, which prides itself upon its scientific achievements and regards religious philanthropy with ill-concealed contempt, is really very unscientific in its acceptance of given social conditions. It builds a few houses for the poor, but does not recognize that an adequate housing scheme for the poor can never be initiated within the limits of private enterprise. Every modern society must come, even if slowly, to the recognition that only a state, armed with the right of eminent domain and able to borrow money at low interest rates, can secure ground and build such houses for the poor as they can afford to buy or rent. In the same way some social workers make elaborate efforts to mitigate the horrors of unemployment, without fully realizing how impossible it is for even the most effective private charity to meet the needs of the unemployed, if the state does not coerce recalcitrant industry to assume its share of this responsibility as a duty, and not as a bit of reluctant generosity. Sometimes the intimate relations of social workers with the wealthy, who are always most prominent in private charity because they are most able to indulge in that luxury, betray them into an easy acceptance of a conservative social philosophy. Social workers who are able to resist the temptation of absorbing the social views of the classes which provide the funds of charity, and who honestly state their social convictions, born of social experience with the needy, such as only a few citizens in a modern society are able to secure, could be of tremendous service to our civilization and to the cause of social readjustment. Social injustice is created not only by greed, but also by social ignorance. If the whole of our society really understood the human consequences of its heedlessness as well as the social worker must understand them, it might be possible to establish a firm foundation for social justice without passing through the chaos and convulsion which now seem inevitable. Since it is impossible, amidst the impersonal relationships of a technological civilization, to achieve such an understanding, those who do have the social experience which most men lack, have a very heavy responsibility upon them. They must make their experience known as widely as possible.

Community workers, at the present moment, are not known for their vigorous social views. Most of them content themselves with the task of alleviating suffering with the resources which are available, without speaking unequivocally to their fellow citizens about the necessity of more adequate methods of social readjustment. Thus social work, in its acceptance of philanthropy as a substitute for real social justice, and for all its scientific pretensions, does not rise very much higher than most sentimental religious generosity.

While the social technicians are trying to keep human sympathy alive amidst the impersonal relations of an industrial civilization, the social scientists are trying to cultivate the intelligence which must guide moral good will. That, too, is a necessary task. Moral good will can express itself automatically in a simple situation, and human sympathy can find an immediate object when relations are intimate. But the intricacies of our technological age demand that good will be guided by an astute intelligence. Ignorant and sentimental America commits itself to the cause of world peace in all kinds of vague gestures, but it is unable to see how its uncompromising attitudes on reparations and war debts is fanning the smoldering flames of war into a new conflagration. In domestic politics we preserve barbaric methods of dealing with unemployment, because we ignorantly fear that a "dole" will cause pauperization, not recognizing that the danger of pauperization inheres in unemployment itself, and not in the adequacy with which we save the unemployed from starvation. We cut wages to overcome the depression, not realizing that low living standards among the multitudes of workers caused the depression in the first place. We raise tariff walls against the trade of other nations, not seeing how national reactions to an international economic situation have caused, and continue to aggravate, the international economic problem. Everywhere human stupidity creates and encourages the national, racial and caste prejudices and bigotries operating as horrible anachronisms within the delicate intricacies of a technological civilization. The social scientists and all the champions of reason are therefore quite right in insisting that the cultivation of a social intelligence, equal to the technical achievements of our age, is an urgent necessity.

Nevertheless, both the social scientists and the social technicians, who try to preserve moral sentiments and to direct them adequately in this kind of world, reveal a certain futility in their sentiments and strategies which are not at all dissimilar to those of the religious idealists who have, through the ages, recoiled at social injustice and expressed their abhorrence thereof by establishing charities. In dealing with the basic problem of social justice—the control of power, the scientists are about as impractical as the religious idealists. The possession of irresponsible power, whether economic or political, makes for injustice, no matter how intelligent the person who wields it. There are occasional benevolent tyrants, but they are never as benevolent as they claim to be, and the consequences of their actions are not even so salutary as their intentions. Usually, whether consciously or unconsciously, their generosities are prompted in part by ulterior motives. They make minor concessions to the

needy in order to hold major advantages; they make
benevolence an occasion for the display of power; or they
hide thereby the severity and mitigate the consequences
of their rule. This is as true of modern industrial auto-
crats as of medieval lords of the manor. It is, in fact,
truer. Power is never quite so unjust, and its rule is
never quite so vexatious, when relations between ruler
and ruled are personal as when they are hidden behind
the impersonal transactions of a moneyed civilization.

The problem of achieving a more adequate social justice, in distinction from the task of making a given social
order as humane as possible, has always been political,
rather than purely moral. That is, it is a problem which
cannot be solved merely by increasing social intelligence
and moral good will, but only by setting the power of the
exploited against the exploiters. In the resulting social
conflict, every degree of social intelligence and moral
good will which social scientists and religious idealists
are able to create, will be so much gain, because it will
mitigate the severities of the conflict. It will make those
who hold inordinate power more inclined to yield it under
pressure, than to meet with threats of violence the social
and political pressure put upon them; and it will prompt
voluntary efforts toward social justice, which may have
an important educational bearing upon the whole situation. Such voluntary efforts—housing schemes for the
poor, coöperative factories, unemployment insurance
schemes—must not, however, be expected to obviate the
necessity for social struggle. The most intelligent and
morally sensitive members of a privileged group may
affect the course of a movement for more equalized jus-

tice, but they cannot eliminate the necessity for political struggle. The failure of Robert Owen to impart his vision of a just society to fellow employers of labor in the last century is a case in point. Yet it cannot be denied that Owen's social idealism did affect, for decades, the temper of the class struggle in England. The larger problems of society are always solved partly by force, and partly by intelligence. There is never sufficient intelligence and idealism to guarantee that the disinherited will gain an increase in rights by waiting for the privileged to divest themselves of their special advantages. Force must be used, though an intelligent society should be able to confine the use of force to those types which operate in the realm of politics, without degenerating into actual violence. The very genius of political force is that it has always possessed certain moral and spiritual elements. Once every degree of moral trust and good will is destroyed among various classes in society, it becomes inevitable that the conflict of power between them should result in violence.

Perhaps no greater issue confronts intellectual and religious idealists, who have tried to preserve and increase the humaneness of modern society, than that of coming to terms with this political problem of justice. Neither have done so thus far. Both have tended to express moral idealism and social good will, only within terms of an established system of society. What they have accomplished could, therefore, always be criticized from an absolute perspective, as being redolent of hypocrisy. Sometimes they have made very rigorous criticisms of the social system itself, but they have naïvely assumed that the system could be changed, merely by the increase of intelligence or religiously inspired good will. They have recoiled at the necessities of a political struggle, and made confusion worse confounded by giving a civilization which is sinking deeper and deeper into social injustice, the impression that only a little more social intelligence would extricate it from its plight.

To a certain degree, the sentimentalities and errors of the social and religious idealists are the natural limitations of the class to which they belong. Their errors belong to the social outlook of the middle classes, who do not understand the inexorable movement of economic power, because they neither wield it nor suffer from it. The middle classes are always politically unrealistic. They view life from the perspective of individual intragroup relationships, where human life reveals itself at its best, and they fail to understand the brutalities of intergroup life. It is significant that they are just as naïve in dealing with international relations, as with the economic relations within a nation. They are always hoping that nations will become as pure in their motives as their individual judges feel themselves to be, and they expect a new educational program to bring this about in the very immediate future.

In as far as the limitations which social workers and religionists betray, are those of the middle classes, they cannot be easily overcome. It is not easy to emancipate oneself from, and to transcend, the limitations which are determined by social experience. A middle-class idealist may have the imagination to see social injustice, and to gauge the human consequences of the disproportion of economic power created by modern society. But he will not feel injustice as keenly as those who actually suffer from it, nor will he have so urgent a social philosophy or strategy as they. If modern civilization fails to achieve a measure of security for the workers, and if it continues to subject them to the horrors of unemployment, they will in time develop a social strategy which will horrify every middle-class idealist. No social philosophy which does not take into consideration the basic differences caused by divergent types of social experience can ever deal realistically with the political problem of social justice. To deal realistically with it, means to be prepared for demands and pressures from the underprivileged, which may go beyond anything envisaged even by the most imaginative members of the more secure community.

The institutions of religion face a particularly difficult problem in dealing with the political issues of modern life. The natural sentiments of religion create a spirit of kindness and philanthropy, but abhor the realities of political struggle. In a static society, it is not impossible to arrive at some adjustment between the religious spirit of love and the political problem of justice. In the social philosophy of Thomas Aquinas, for instance, the spirit of generosity and love overarches the system of justice, and adds the grace of personal kindness to the scheme of justice established by the state. But, in his day, inequality was taken for granted, and the differences in privilege among the various classes did not affront the conscience of anyone. In our day, equal justice is not only demanded by an advancing moral logic which destroys with inexorable consistency all the specious defenses of special privilege, but it is made necessary by a productive process which is reduced by inequality to anarchy. Humanity is never so sensitive morally as to insist upon perfect justice; and those who suffer from injustice are never so impatient with what they suffer as to demand the absolute, if their condition is at all bearable. The reason equalitarianism becomes a more and more compelling social philosophy, in an industrial civilization, is that inequality in the distribution of wealth periodically reduces the whole scheme of production to chaos. Social injustice has become economically unfeasible. If millions of workers do not receive an adequate portion of the wealth of industry, they lack the buying power to absorb the goods of industry. The fact that they may actually have higher living standards in periods of prosperity than workers of pre-industrial periods, does not save them from periods of terrible insecurity when the markets of the world are glutted with goods. It is the insecurity of periods of overproduction which makes the problem of social justice so much more urgent than it has been in any other era of history, and which drives modern society either to equal justice or to chaos.

Since equal justice cannot be achieved without political struggle, and since religious idealism, relying upon spontaneous impulses and frowning upon the exact measurements of "mine" and "thine" which every adequate social ethic must use, is peculiarly awkward in its approach to the ethico-political problem, the modern church is in a most difficult situation and cannot easily preserve the natural fruits of its spirit from the corruption of hypocrisy and self-deception. If the moral idealism of the Christian church can issue in nothing but naïve philanthropy, the church will not be able to maintain any significant moral prestige in the modern community. On the other hand, there will probably never be a time when it will not be desirable to cultivate personal kindness and generosity. Only the most extreme romanticists hope for a day in which the political reorganization of society will solve all social problems, obviating the necessity for imaginative and unselfish concern for the needs of our fellow men.

If the church is wise, it may be able to solve the problem of this conflict between the religious ideal of love and the political ideal of justice. It will make a vigorous analysis of the economic and political sources of social need, so that no one who tries to alleviate immediate need will rest under the illusion that such generosity obviates the necessity for the elimination of the economic sources of social need. It will care for the unemployed, for instance, but will use the occasion to instruct its members in the basic causes of unemployment. It will make them conscious of the perils of power to those who wield it, and to the society which permits irresponsible power to remain unchecked. It will help its members not only to analyze society objectively, but to analyze themselves. If it does this honestly, it will persuade kind people that there is always an element of the assertion of power in the expression of pity. It will help the philanthropist, who, as Jesus observed, gives of "his superfluity," to realize that he is not quite as unselfish as he seems to be. It will thus reduce the moral conceit which is the inevitable by-product of all philanthropic ventures, and in fact of all moral achievement.

There is no reason why religion should not deal more rigorously with the psychological and economic problems which underlie our social maladjustments. If it has difficulty in analyzing the social scene, it ought to have no such difficulty in the psychological analysis of human greed and selfishness. Vital religion has always been rather astute in its insights into the motives of the human heart. It has insisted that men are selfish, when more sentimental observers were impressed by their unselfishness. It ought, therefore, to be able to deal realistically with the motives which express themselves in philanthropy, and to separate the precious from the vile. If modern religion is extremely sentimental in accepting every philanthropic gesture as the last word in the expression of the Christian spirit, that is partly because it has imbibed the general sentimentality of modern culture. True religion prompts to both love and humility, and the humility preserves the unselfish man from assuming that he is unselfish. If he is truly religious, both the insights of the past and a knowledge of himself will help him to realize how much of selfishness is always compounded with unselfishness in the generous deed. The truly religious man does know himself as no one else does. He is an adept at profound introspection, and the criteria with which he approaches the task of introspection are those which have the touch of perfection upon them. He feels himself falling short of the holiness of God. Unfortunately, religion can be used more easily to encourage moral conceit, than to produce moral humility.

For it is only religion at first-hand that prompts to humility. Second-hand religion easily sanctifies conventional virtues as final revelations of the will of God. Wherever the church achieves a really vital religion, it is able to mitigate the animosities of the social struggle by robbing the privileged classes of the moral conceit which is one of their chief weapons, as well as a principal cause of their political intransigeance.

Religion at its best can make another contribution to the cause of social justice. The religious ideal, the absolute conceived as the goal of history, is not only a personal ideal, but a social one. Religion has always dreamt of the Kingdom of God. It has always believed in some kind of millennium. Only the extreme individualism of middle-class religion, in the past two centuries, has narrowed the religious vision to the individual life, and made personal immortality and perfection the sole goal of religious striving. In the religion of the prophets and in the gospel of Jesus, there is a vision of a redeemed society. It is very probable that the political means necessary for the achievement of a just society have never been clearly envisaged by any religion. It was always expected that the social redemption would come by divine intervention, though it must be noted that not infrequently the intervention was conceived of in political terms. God was to use the wrath of man to praise him, and to make Assyrians and Egyptians the tools of his purposes. Religion has, of course, always had a moral ideal which proceded from a sensitive individual conscience, rather than from the life of the group. It meant that ideal to be applicable for the group, however. Jesus' ideal of love is probably too high for the attainment of any nation. No nation, or any other group for that matter, will ever sacrifice itself for another. The perfect ideal for the individual is too high for intergroup relations. Groups will do well to approximate justice, rather than love. But the perfection of the religious goal can be instrumental in prompting the religious man to assume a highly critical attitude toward all contemporary social arrangements: they fall short of the kingdom of God.

If middle-class religion has lost the vision of a redeemed society and become obsessed with the purely individual aspects of religion, we may always count on the disinherited to restore that vision. In modern proletarianism, in which the apocalyptic vision is very apparent, there are some characteristics which separate it definitely from classical, or historic, religion. The cynicism of proletarianism is probably inevitable, but it springs from the fact that it derives its insights into human nature entirely from the dismal facts of intergroup relations, and does not see what is best in human nature. It tends therefore to underestimate the moral forces which are actually at work in human life, and to overemphasize the brutal factors. This tendency in proletarian religion will be worked out to its logical conclusion, if middle-class culture and religion do not overcome their sentimentality, and if they do not learn to deal realistically with politico-moral problems.

Whatever may be the weaknesses of proletarian religion, it does have the vision of a just society to spur human effort, and the tremendous moral energy which that vision inspires is proof of the fact that men do not move toward high goals without religious passion. Their religion may be good or bad, judged from varying perspectives, but like all vital religions, it does create an energy which is beyond the capacities of rationalists. That fact can best be proved by comparing a modern communist, with his almost demoniac passion, with a typical intellectual liberal. If a new society is to be built, we may be sure that religion will have a hand in building it. Only religion has the power to destroy the old and to build the new. Whether that new creative religion will be absolutely destructive of the values incorporated in classical religion, or whether it will learn how to appropriate what is best in the insights of the past for its own uses, will depend to a large degree upon the ability of classical religion to come to terms with the ethico-political problem of modern industrial society, out of which proletarian religion is being born.

The Christian religion is compounded of insights which develop in individual life, and those which emerge out of social life. The individual insights, the religious feelings which men have when they face, in loneliness of spirit, the eternal mystery of life, and look into the profundities of their own souls with both gratitude and contrition—these are as lacking among industrial workers who face an urgent social situation and whose necessities have forced a communal spirit upon them, as the insights of social religion are usually lost in middle-class religion. The middle-class person is an individual who is not conscious of either the joys or the atrocities of intensive communal life. He is too self-sufficient to feel himself dependent upon the group, and too comfortable

BIBLIOGRAPHY

BIBLIOGRAPHY

I

CLEMENT of ALEXANDRIA, Pædagogus.

DÖLLINGER, JOHANN J. I. VON, Die Reformation, Regensburg, 1846.

LECKY, W. E. H., History of European Morals from Augustus to Charlemagne, New York, 1929.

ORIGEN, Leviticum Homilia.

TERTULLIAN, Apologiticus.

UHLHORN, GERHARD, Christian Charity in the Ancient Church, New York, 1883.

Vita Sancti Cypriani, Migne's Patrologia Latinas.

II

GRAY, B. K., History of English Philanthropy, London, 1905.

KIRK, KENNETH E., The Vision of God, New York, 1931.

LECKY, W. E. H., History of European Morals from Augustus to Charlemagne, New York, 1929.

NELSON, ROBERT, Address to Persons of Quality and Estate, 1715.

UHLHORN, GERHARD, Christian Charity in the Ancient Church, New York, 1883.

TROELTSCH, ERNST, The Social Teaching of the Christian Church. Translated by Olive Wyon, New York, 1931.

III

EDMAN, IRWIN, The Contemporary and His Soul, New York, 1931.

HADFIELD, JAMES A., The Psychology of Power, New York, 1923.

HINKLE, BEATRICE M., The Recreating of the Individual, New York, 1923.

IV

JAMES, WILLIAM, Varieties of Religious Experience, New York, 1902.

MOORE, THOMAS Y., Dynamic Psychology, Philadelphia, 1926.

V

BABBITT, IRVING, Rousseau and Romanticism, New York, 1930.

KRUTCH, JOSEPH WOOD, The Modern Temper, New York, 1929.

INDEX

INDEX

COLUMBIA UNIVERSITY PRESS
Columbia University
New York

———

foreign agent
OXFORD UNIVERSITY PRESS
Humphrey Milford
Amen House, London, E. C.